RUNNING
—the sacred art

RUNNING
—the sacred art

preparing
to practice

Dr. Warren A. Kay

Foreword by Kristin Armstrong

Walking Together, Finding the Way®
SKYLIGHT PATHS®
PUBLISHING
Woodstock, Vermont

Running—The Sacred Art:
Preparing to Practice

2007 First Printing
© 2007 by Warren A. Kay
Foreword © 2007 by Kristin Armstrong

Frontispiece courtesy of Villanova University Archives, Villanova, PA

Library of Congress Cataloging-in-Publication Data
Kay, Warren A.
Running—the sacred art : preparing to practice / Warren A. Kay ; foreword by Kristin Armstrong.
     p. cm. — (The art of spiritual living)
Includes bibliographical references.
ISBN-13: 978-1-59473-227-0 (quality pbk.)
ISBN-10: 1-59473-227-2 (quality pbk.)
   1. Running—Religious aspects. 2. Runners (Sports)—Religious life. 3. Spiritual life. I. Title. II. Title: Running.
BL629.5.R85.K39 2007
204'.46—dc22
                                                                                2007035153

10 9 8 7 6 5 4 3 2 1

Manufactured in the United States of America
Cover Design: Jenny Buono

SkyLight Paths Publishing is creating a place where people of different spiritual traditions come together for challenge and inspiration, a place where we can help each other understand the mystery that lies at the heart of our existence.

SkyLight Paths sees both believers and seekers as a community that increasingly transcends traditional boundaries of religion and denomination—people wanting to learn from each other, *walking together, finding the way.*

SkyLight Paths, "Walking Together, Finding the Way" and colophon are trademarks of LongHill Partners, Inc., registered in the U.S. Patent and Trademark Office.

Walking Together, Finding the Way®
Published by SkyLight Paths Publishing
A Division of LongHill Partners, Inc.
Sunset Farm Offices, Route 4, P.O. Box 237
Woodstock, VT 05091
Tel: (802) 457-4000   Fax: (802) 457-4004
www.skylightpaths.com

We run, not because we think it is doing us good, but because we enjoy it and cannot help ourselves.... The more restricted our society and work become, the more necessary it will be to find some outlet for this craving for freedom.

—*Roger Bannister,* The First Four Minutes

If I find in myself a desire which no experience in this world can satisfy, the most probable explanation is that I was made for another world. If none of my earthly pleasures satisfy it, that does not prove that the universe is a fraud. Probably earthly pleasures were never meant to satisfy it, but only to arouse it, to suggest the real thing.

—*C. S. Lewis,* Mere Christianity

CONTENTS

FOREWORD

When I cook a meal, I cannot tell you what is most meaningful or enjoyable to me: thoughtfully planning the meal, thumbing through cookbooks, making lists and leisurely shopping for ingredients, preparing the meal, setting the table, welcoming friends, uncorking the wine, completing the final touches, serving the meal, saying grace, enjoying the food, or lingering in conversation at the table deep into the evening.

It is much the same for me about running. I cannot separate the act from the meaning, the physical from the spiritual, or the metaphors from the monotony. It is an area in my life where the different planes of my existence are thoroughly and delightfully fused. Although I am a contributing editor for a major magazine (*Runner's World*) I cannot write with depth and integrity about this subject of sport and exclude my faith. It is very likely that I would have been fired or at least chastised by now for my spiritual openness (I say with a smile), if the spiritual element inherent in running did not resonate with so many runners and readers.

When running begins to shift from a painful pastime into a beloved passion, those who don't understand might think that we are obsessively and obtusely running away. I disagree. When that shift happened for me as a runner, I felt awareness settle into my stride that I was not running from anything. Rather I was running *toward something*. As Warren Kay points out in his inspiring guide to running as a spiritual practice, this essential difference encapsulates everything it means to be a spiritual runner. I was (and still am) running toward a higher and richer understanding of myself, of my friends, and of God.

At a dark time in my life when I was lacking peace and clarity, I began to read about meditation. I longed to be one of those people who could achieve peace through meditation—quiet my mind, calm my heart by focusing on my breath or repeating a mantra. But I could never quite make that happen by sitting still, my thoughts buzzing around annoyingly like summer insects by an outside light. Bless the person who wrote something that I read someplace that said it was possible to enter a state of meditation by monotonous movement. This is my sacred space when I run alone, this is my ritual, this is my sanctuary! I find God here, waiting for me, matching my pace. As my breath gets less jagged and my stride settles into my unique pattern of effort, I find inner stillness cradled in outer motion. Through that stillness I have found a great deal of peace. After a lifetime of panting, I finally caught my breath.

In the midst of that same dark time, two of my friends took notice of my haggard appearance—the dark circles under my eyes, and the brittle countenance of a woman without appetite. They, being lifetime runners, knew what I needed before I did. They knew that I needed to gain the confidence of knowing I could work through pain on a physical level so that I could face the work ahead of me on emotional and spiritual levels. They were wise and compassionate company in my pilgrimage out of despair. In helping me train for my first marathon they gave me a precious gift. With God's help working through them, I ran my way out of the pit and back to my passion and purpose, my faith and my writing. I finally had the courage to put the speaking voice of my heart and my head onto paper. I am becoming my true self.

For me, running was a catalyst for healing on all levels. I still run with these same incredible women, and our early morning runs have become our touchstone. Our miles logged together have carried us across emotional and spiritual chasms and have solidified friendships deeper and more authentic than any I have ever known. We sweat together, we suffer together, we persevere together, we pray together, and we believe together—in each other, in ourselves, and in an almighty God.

We are blessed, indeed.

People of faith talk a lot about the journey, about what it means to "walk with God." We are all sojourners together on a path, regardless of how we regard our itinerary. This way of thinking is perfectly exemplified to me whether it is the start line of a race, the act of lining up on the track, or the gathering of girl-friends pre-dawn, stretching and waiting to begin. We are all on this journey together and if we can draw deeper meaning from our miles, we will find that we are well trained in every capacity for whatever lies ahead.

Oswald Chambers describes this better than I can, in his famous work *My Utmost for His Highest*. He describes the need to do our work in the workroom or else when crisis comes we will be of no use to ourselves, and likely a hindrance to those in our care. Crisis might come at mile twenty-one of a marathon; it might come in the form of a severed relationship, the loss of employment, a betrayal, a severe setback or disappointment, or bad news from the doctor. The form it may take is a mystery; that it will come is a certainty. Running is a perfect illustration of the workroom. As we run we train our bodies, minds, and spirits, and our fitness levels in each category rise accordingly. When we find ourselves or a loved one in crisis, face to face with a heavy burden, we can carry it with grace, strength, and endurance.

Spiritual fitness and freedom are closely aligned. Today's society tells us we need to have more, have it better, and have it faster. But society can't tell us what it is we need. And so we press on at warp speed in a race to acquire and achieve. We strive and we strain, and yet so many of us come up empty, restless. We require something different, something deeper. We were created to need connection, created with a longing for the freedom to be understood and to understand. This need can only be filled in spiritual terms, from a reservoir of an unseen Source.

And this is my wish for you, my friend, fellow runner, fellow traveler, that you would find that reservoir, and this book can serve as your map. It will help you realize that your spiritual source is already present, well within the grasp of your understanding, just beneath the surface of your everyday life, residing in the place inside you that longs for acknowledgement and release. Freedom awaits. Now put your shoes on and go find it.

Blessings over all your miles,
Kristin Armstrong

Therefore since we are surrounded by such a great cloud of witnesses, let us throw off everything that hinders and the sin that so easily entangles and let us run with perseverance the race marked out for us.
Hebrews 12:1

INTRODUCTION

Running to him was real, the way he did it the realest thing he knew. It was all joy and woe, hard as diamond; it made him weary beyond comprehension. But it also made him free.

—*John L. Parker Jr.,* Once a Runner[1]

"Whenever I find myself growing grim about the mouth," says Ishmael, in the well-known opening of Moby-Dick, "whenever it is a damp, drizzly November of the soul ... I account it high time to get to sea as soon as I can." Couldn't Ishmael have just gone for a run instead?

—*John Jerome,* The Elements of Effort[2]

In the summer Olympic Games of 1956 held in Melbourne, Australia, the final heat of the 1,500-meter run included John Landy of Australia as the favorite to win. Landy had had a stellar career up to that point, being the second person in history to break the four-minute barrier in the mile (the first person to break it was Roger Bannister at Oxford University in 1954). Included in that final heat was Irishman Ron Delaney, also an accomplished middle-distance runner. As the race entered the final lap, John Landy and Ron Delaney were running together at around tenth place, but they were only 6 meters off the lead. Known for having a devastating kick, Delaney waited through the next turn, and as they went into the back straight, he made his move, passing the field. With less than a hundred meters left in the race, he felt like he was flying and later commented, "I don't think I have ever felt as good." Delaney crossed the line in first place (Landy finished third) in a new Olympic record of 3:41.2. Then the reality of what happened quickly sunk in, and he spontaneously flopped down on the side of the track, hands clasped in a prayer of thanksgiving to God. The photograph at the front of this book records that very moment. Several days later, Ron Delaney flew back to the United States to continue his studies at Villanova University, just outside of Philadelphia.[3]

Fourteen years later, I entered Villanova University as a freshman. In the field house (the old gym on campus that was built back in 1932), there hung a large copy of that same photograph. I had known about Ron Delaney before I ever attended Villanova, but had never heard the story of his prayer after winning Olympic gold. I remember the first time I saw the picture with its caption describing the event—I was in awe. I was a religious person and a runner, too. Here was a public demonstration by someone who was a runner and also deeply spiritual. Over the next four years, I passed that picture often, and I seldom went by it without pausing to gaze at this great runner in his humble gesture of thankfulness to God. Although I never approached the accomplishments of such great runners as Ron Delaney, I was inspired by that photograph and what it represented—and still represents—to me. I have always enjoyed running—both competitively and recreationally—but seeing that photograph of Ron Delaney was for me the beginning of *spiritual* running.

THE RUNNING OBSESSION

Fast-forward many years and thousands of miles of running. Today I am a professor at a small New England college where I also am a coach of the cross-country and track teams—and I still love to run. The other day I went into a bookstore and came across a book with the title *Wired to Run: The Runaholics Anonymous Guide to Living with Running Addiction*. Although the book is intended to be funny, the obsession it deals with—running—is real. Since the mid-1960s and 1970s, more and more people have been putting on their running shoes and taking to the roads—alone or in groups, to lose weight or just to keep fit, and even for competition. More and more cities are hosting marathons—and it's big business. People definitely are hooked on running, and it doesn't look like it is going to ease up. And there is a reason for that. The two quotations at the beginning of this introduction express a very real and pervasive attitude toward running. The first one is from one of my favorite books of all time—*Once a Runner* by John Parker. It expresses the feeling many of us have that running does something that nothing else can do, and although at times it is difficult, it also allows us to be *free*. In a world where we have so many responsibilities and cares, we *can* do something that helps us overcome those feelings of anxiety and stress—we can run! The second quotation, from writer and runner John Jerome, expresses in its own way much the same idea. And if you ask me, it is true. Running—for those of us who do it regularly—helps us deal with life; it helps us cope with problems and celebrate triumphs. You may not even know why it helps, it just does. In the following pages I hope you will be able to discover some of the reasons why—reasons that are right for you.

RUNNING IS THE NEW YOGA

This is a book about running and spirituality. There was a time when combining these two concepts would have seemed strange to most people, but today more and more people are aware that this is a natural combination whose time has come.

In fact, many have made favorable comparisons between running and yoga. Thousands of years ago, yoga developed as a spiritual discipline—a system of body and mind control—in the religions of Hinduism and Buddhism. The person who practices yoga exercises the body, stretching it into a variety of often difficult postures. And by doing this, one strives to achieve enlightenment—liberation of the self from illusion, and ultimately, union with the Divine. Back in the 1950s and 1960s, yoga was little known in this country, and it was thought of as a primarily religious activity. Then people began to recognize the health benefits of yoga. Gradually, it gained acceptance as a form of physical exercise. Today I think you would be hard-pressed to find a gym or health spa in the country that doesn't also offer yoga lessons, yet for most people who practice yoga, the spiritual side has been minimized or even ignored.

Nearly the same things can be said about running—but the other way around. Since the 1960s and 1970s, jogging and running have been recognized as a terrific form of exercise. The "running revolution," as some people call it, began in the 1960s and was heavily influenced by Coach Bill Bowerman of the University of Oregon. Although Bowerman is best known as the coach of Steve Prefontaine and as the founder of the running shoe company Nike, his influence on the running revolution came through a book he wrote with Dr. Waldo Harris—*Jogging: Medically Approved Physical Fitness Program for All Ages* (1967). In that little book, the authors emphasized the health benefits of running. Since that time, a flood of literature has supported that claim. Running does, indeed, provide an efficient way to burn calories for weight loss; it helps tone muscle and is great for cardiovascular health. But recently, men and women across the country have recognized that, like yoga, running can also be a *spiritual* exercise—a means to spiritual enlightenment or spiritual fulfillment.

ASPECTS OF SPIRITUAL HEALTH

We live in a fast-food society that doesn't always promote a healthy lifestyle. We also live in a materialistic society that does not always promote spiritual health. In this book, I will address the three main aspects of spirituality and spiritual health. First, spirituality is concerned with establishing a right relationship with ourselves. To put it simply, many people are just not at home with themselves. As human beings, we are often disappointed with who we are. Sometimes we feel this way because of things we have or have not done, but often, it is just a nagging feeling we have for no apparent reason. We are not alone in this. Most of us know people who seem to have it all—good looks, money, relationships—but something in their lives is missing, and they are not happy. That is a spiritual problem.

Second, healthy spirituality involves good relationships with other people. We live in a society where people often think of themselves primarily in terms of possessions and material wealth. For many people, success is defined by dollars and cents, not by the quality of personal relationships. Some people even take this a step further, thinking of other people as commodities. They are only interested in a potential relationship to the extent that they can profit from it. That also is a spiritual problem.

And third, true spirituality is concerned with fostering a good and healthy relationship with the Divine or sacred reality, or what I, myself, as a Christian refer to as God. This book is written with the conviction that running *can* help promote a healthy spirituality in all three of these areas.

Motive, Opportunity, and Means

I suppose we have all watched enough police and detective television shows to know that any good criminal court case is comprised of three essential elements: motive, opportunity, and means. I believe that these same three elements enter into achieving a healthy spirituality as I describe it in this book. We need to find the proper *motivation* and create the right *opportunities* to make the effort, and perhaps most important, we need to find the *means* to achieve our goal.

If you have picked up this book and have read this far, you are already motivated to investigate the spirituality of running. Perhaps you are a runner who feels alienated from yourself or out of place in society, and since going for a run is a time when you feel good about yourself, you want to learn how you can take that experience further. Perhaps you feel that there is a God, and even though you've been dissatisfied with organized religion, you still crave a place where you can feed your soul. Whatever your reason, you have the *motivation*.

If you are already a runner you know that distance running gives you the *opportunity* to do a lot of thinking. Now you can use that opportunity to do what is necessary to help your situation. When you go out for a run—even for a few miles—it gives you some time to step back from the rat race of life. After all, when we run we are taking time away from the routine that often has a numbing effect on us.

Finally, there is a growing consensus among practitioners that running, when done properly, helps us feel good physically, mentally, and spiritually. In ways that no other activity can do, running helps us feel free. And with the motive and the opportunity in place, and this book in hand, you now have at your disposal a very practical guide to discover the means to true spiritual running.

A Spiritual Journal

Most serious runners already realize how important it is to keep a running journal (some may call it a log or a diary). But few people understand that it is equally important for the spiritual runner to keep one as well. My one journal does double duty as both a running and a spiritual journal. This invaluable tool does not have to be very fancy. Mine is a simple notebook in which I keep a record of how far I ran, what the conditions were, how I felt, and how long it took me. This information serves a number of functions. First, it helps me be accurate and consistent because my memory sometimes plays tricks on me, as it can with anyone ("Did I run four or five times this week?"). Second, it can also help illuminate causes and effects that would have otherwise gone unnoticed in case something goes wrong. So, for example, if I get a pain in my knee, I can review what I was doing on my runs in the days and weeks before and perhaps adjust my routine to avoid the same pain in the future.

> "The log is a motivator and an enforcer. The simple act of writing down your mileage is motivational. After several weeks you'll find yourself looking back through it to find reasons for 'bad' days."
> —Jeff Galloway,[4] *Galloway's Book on Running*

The spiritual part of my running journal is equally helpful in some of the same ways. Consistency is a significant factor for progress in spiritual running, and keeping a spiritual journal can help. Writing down your own spiritual observations made during a run will help you remember them next time, and the journal can assist you in keeping track of spiritual health. A spiritual running journal can also provide a constant source of motivational and inspirational quotations, thoughts, and sayings. Reading it can help you on your runs by being the basis for your own private spiritual pep talk, much like coaches give their teams before big games.

So in a sense, the activity of running and then writing in the spiritual journal forms a circular movement, illustrated in the diagram on the next page. When you run, you may have experiences that you can write down in your spiritual journal, then the spiritual journal provides inspiration and motivation the next time you run. But remember, although you get in shape by running in an effort to run even farther, the health benefits you get from running extend to all areas of your life. In the same way, although the spiritual journal helps you get motivated to run, the spiritual benefits of this entire exercise have the potential to affect your whole life, too. Feeling better about yourself can help you work better and interact better with friends and associates.

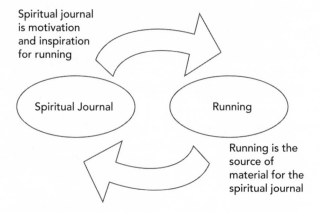

Spiritual journal is motivation and inspiration for running

Spiritual Journal

Running

Running is the source of material for the spiritual journal

Getting Started on Your Spiritual Running Journal

Writing can also be a form of spirituality. Throughout this book, I will be suggesting specific exercises to help you begin to apply the principles discussed, and most of these exercises will involve writing in your spiritual journal. So let's get started.

Take some time to consider how you feel about the three aspects of spiritual health I talked about earlier in this chapter:

- Having a right relationship with ourselves
- Having a right relationship with other people
- Having a right relationship with the Divine

It might be helpful to go into a quiet room where you are not likely to be disturbed to think about this. Alternatively, you could use your next run to think about these aspects of spiritual health, but, try to pick a route without a lot of cars, people, or other distractions.

On a piece of paper or in a notebook, which will become your spiritual journal, write down at least three things about each of the aspects of spirituality that you *are not* happy with or that could be improved and also three things that you *are* happy with. If you find it hard to name even three things to be happy about concerning your spirituality, that's all right—that's why you are reading this book. Take your time when you do this; after all, this is going to be the first entry in your private journal, and you don't have to show it to anyone. If you don't want to do all three aspects at once, focus on one area of spirituality and write down at least five specific things about yourself that you want to improve.

If you are really serious about spiritual running, every time you go out for a run (at least until you get further into this book) read one or two of those points you have written down and think about them while you run. But don't expect a lot to change right away. At this point, you are only thinking about aspects of your own spirituality that you are not happy with and aspects that you are happy with. But thinking about them as you run will help you clarify them in your mind. Even though there are negative things, don't let them get you down—be positive! They are simply areas where you have identified opportunities for growth. As you read through this book and as you run, you will be a more spiritual person in the process—and always remember that it is a continual process.

METAPHOR OR METHOD

One of the greatest running movies of all time is without a doubt the 1981 classic *Chariots of Fire*. Not only does it tell a great story, but the theme music by Vangelis has also been inspiring runners for more than twenty-five years. The movie is based on the true story of the British Olympic track team of 1924. One of the movie's main characters is Eric Liddell, a devout Christian from Scotland who later became a missionary to China. Eric is definitely a spiritual runner, at one point in the movie telling his sister, "I believe God made me for a purpose, but he also made me fast. And when I run I feel his pleasure." Liddell was well known throughout all of Scotland, and he used his fame as an athlete to attract people to meetings where he could share with them the Christian message. In one scene in *Chariots of Fire*, after he had just won his race in a track meet against Ireland (about twenty-five minutes into the movie), he gives a brief sermon to a crowd of spectators. He begins the sermon with the following words:

> You came to see a race today, to see someone win. It happened to be me. But I want you to do more than just watch a race. I want you to take part in it. I want to compare faith to running in a race. It's hard. It requires concentration of will; energy of soul.... I have no formula for winning the race. Everyone runs in her own way or his own way. And where does the power come from to see the race to its end? From within....

Here, Liddell uses running as a metaphor. He is comparing the Christian way of life to running in a race—an interesting and fruitful comparison. But using running as a metaphor for the religious life didn't begin with Eric Liddell. Running, and running a race, are popular images in the New Testament as well.

The metaphorical approach is perfectly valid in any discussion of spirituality. But for the most part, it is not the approach I take on this topic. I advocate the use of running as a *method*—a physical discipline to be used by anyone who wishes to explore the realm of spirituality. Some people go to church every day. I think we can just as well go for a run!

IS RUNNING AN ART?

You may have wondered why a book on running is in a series called The Art of Spiritual Living. There are at least three things that make this appropriate. First, art is a discipline. To be really good at an art form, you have to be disciplined in the process of learning and developing the techniques needed to produce the art. In a similar way, no one can just go out there and run a marathon. It takes training—long hours of running and working out. And achieving a healthy spiritual life takes discipline, too. Don't think of spirituality as something that you can achieve overnight. It takes determination and discipline.

Second, art takes skill. A person has to possess the necessary skills to excel at a particular art form. Similarly, running is a skill. Running is more than just putting one foot in front of the other in rapid succession. Even for those who are good at running, it takes discipline and dedication to develop the skill. And spirituality is more than thinking good thoughts—it takes skill as well, like contemplation and meditation. We will develop these skills on the following pages.

Finally, art takes dedication. I don't believe anyone who ever succeeded as an artist lacked the necessary commitment to his or her art. Running takes dedication as well. The most successful runners at any level are people who are devoted to their sport. And to be a spiritual person involves dedication, as we shall see.

THIS BOOK IS FOR ALL SORTS OF RUNNERS

I have consciously written this book with a number of different types of people in mind. Many people in this country run, and they run for a variety of reasons. But a large percentage of these people believe there is a spiritual benefit to be gained through running. If this includes you, then this book is definitely for you.

As we proceed in this study, you will need to examine some of your basic beliefs. These beliefs form the starting points for developing your own spirituality of running. I am a Christian and base my spirituality on a belief in one God who created the world. As such, the spirituality I practice is similar in many respects to the spirituality of Judaism and Islam, since these religions have in common with Christianity belief in one God.

This book is also for the nonreligious person; that is, the person who doesn't have any specific religious beliefs but who acknowledges that there is more to the world than just what we can see, feel, hear, or investigate with science. Similarly, this book is for the person who is dissatisfied or even bored with traditional forms of religion and spirituality. For many people, going to organized religious services has become a routine without meaning. And last, this book is also for those who just want to use their love of running in spiritually productive ways.

As you read this book, it might be helpful to think of it in the same way you think about going for a run. On the one hand, it takes a certain amount of time and discipline to get through it (not too much, I hope). On the other hand, when you're through, you'll feel better because you will have learned something that will help you maximize your running experience.

After years of reading books by famous runners and well-known writers on running, I have gathered numerous informative, inspirational, and motivational quotations that are, for the most part, not spiritual in nature. I have distributed a number of these quotations throughout this book for a couple of reasons. First, I would like to inform less-experienced runners and remind seasoned runners of some basic principles of running. Second, I hope some of these passages will inspire and motivate runners of all sorts.[5]

In what follows it is not my intention to mystify anyone. True spirituality should be available to everyone regardless of education or background, and I don't want to hide behind big, fancy words. Religion (or spirituality) is a part of who we are as human beings. In the history of humankind, no society has been without religion or a spirituality of some sort—despite the attempts of some people or groups to ridicule or eradicate it. But even though spirituality can and should be accessible to everybody, that doesn't mean that it is necessarily easy. There's no doubt about it, running can be challenging at times, even for the most gifted runner. The good news is that running is also a lot of fun—and the sacred art of running can be, too!

LET'S GET A FEW THINGS STRAIGHT

Write the vision; make it plain upon tablets,
so he may run who reads it.

—Habakkuk 2:2 (RSV)[1]

I was in a secondhand bookstore a few weeks ago when I came across a classic—*The Complete Book of Running* by Jim Fixx.[2] This great book helped fuel the running revolution in the 1970s. Fixx started out a very unlikely athlete: he was overweight, and a smoker. He was also smart. *Really* smart. In fact, he was a member of Mensa, a club for people with very high IQs. He was also a good writer, and when he graduated from Oberlin College, he became a professional writer who contributed to some prominent national magazines and even published a number of books for smart people, such as *Games for the Super-Intelligent*, *More Games for the Super-Intelligent*, and *Solve It!* But in 1977, Jim Fixx published *The Complete Book of Running*, which influenced the history of American culture in some pretty amazing ways.

Interest in running had started for Fixx ten years earlier, in 1967. He weighed 214 pounds and smoked heavily. He didn't feel good, and he wanted to get healthy, so he took up running. By the time *The Complete Book of Running* was published, Jim had lost 60 pounds and quit smoking, and he felt great. The book informed its readers of the benefits of running as a form of physical exercise. It became a huge success and soared to the top of the bestseller list, where it stayed for eleven weeks, eventually selling more than a million copies. In 1980, Fixx wrote a sequel titled *Jim Fixx's Second Book of Running: The Companion Volume to the Complete Book of Running*.[3]

But tragedy struck in the summer of 1984. At age fifty-two, during one of his daily runs, Jim Fixx suffered a massive heart attack and died. Cholesterol had partially blocked three of his arteries. Some people blamed running for his death and claimed that this was proof of the harmful effects of running.

When I found Jim Fixx's book in the bookstore, I wanted to buy it because I had lost my copy years ago. But when I opened the book to see how much it cost, the bookstore owner had written the following words where the price should have been: "A lot of good it did him."

What that bookstore owner didn't know was that Jim Fixx had a family history of heart disease. His father had died at the age of forty-two. And given his own unhealthy lifestyle for his first thirty-five years, many have convincingly argued that Jim Fixx actually added years to his life through running. But more than just adding years to his life, Fixx improved the *quality* of his life. Running guru and author George Sheehan, MD, wrote in his book *Running and Being: The Total Experience,* "Don't be concerned if running or exercise will add years to your life, be concerned with adding life to your years."[4] Jim Fixx is one of the best examples I know of someone who lived just that way. He did it with his running, and that is something that we all have the potential of doing when we take up the sport of regular running.

> "Don't judge your running by your speed. Judge it by how you feel and what your doctor tells you."
> —Amby Burfoot,[5] *The Principles of Running: Practical Lessons from My First 100,000 Miles*

Not only did Jim Fixx improve the quality of his own life, but he has also helped countless others improve theirs. The number of people who are active runners has increased dramatically since the 1970s and 1980s in large part due to the publication of his books. But there is a lesson to be learned from all of this as well: when considering increasing strenuous activity, especially as you get older or when it involves a sudden change in lifestyle, you should consult a physician before you begin.

No Fast-Food Spirituality

Families used to spend hours preparing and cooking meals, but now a growing number of people are turning to fast-food restaurants where all they need to do is stop at a drive-through window and pick up any amount of food at any time of day—almost instantly. The appeal of this newer option has led many to say that we have become a "fast-food nation."[6] And it is not limited to the way we eat. In addition to fast food, many people now insist on driving everywhere they want to go rather than walking—even when it is only a few blocks.

Perhaps not surprisingly, this mentality has extended to religion and spirituality as well. In the 1950s, people began going to drive-in *churches*. The trend started in California, where one innovative minister preached every Sunday at a drive-in movie theater. There, people drove to "church," listened to the sermon through the little speakers at each parking space, and nobody had to get out of the car at all. One such church developed the following slogan, which appealed to many people: "Worship as you are ... in the family car."[7] So it has even come to that—fast-food spirituality!

The spirituality that I am proposing on these pages is different than the organized institutional religion that has developed in this country; it harkens back to a more basic way of being spiritual. For thousands of years, spiritual practices from around the world have been referred to as spiritual *disciplines*—and that implies effort. To be a good runner at any level is not easy or convenient; you have to take the time to run miles and miles each week, even occasionally when you don't feel like running. Running as a spiritual discipline requires effort as well. No fast-food spirituality here!

Since spirituality is concerned with fostering a right relationship with ourselves, with others, and with God, the spirituality of running is an attempt to eliminate any factors that may get in the way of an honest confrontation with each of these three elements. First, running provides a unique opportunity to experience ourselves differently than we normally do. We are not surrounded by our possessions by which we judge ourselves and our worth and are judged by others. When we run, we experience ourselves with all our strengths and shortcomings and are not distracted by those other external factors.

Second, as runners we are part of a community of like-minded individuals. Not far from where I live, there is a bicycle trail where I like to run when the weather is nice. I usually run about four or five miles in one direction before turning around and running back. Along the way, I pass many other people who are running, walking, roller-skating, or biking on the path. I experience the other people running on the path differently than I would if I encountered them wearing their fancy (or not so fancy) clothes and surrounded by their possessions and other things by which they define themselves and are defined by others. The encounter with other runners, as fellow runners, is most often an encounter with friends: friends we have never met before and friends we may not even know by name—but friends nonetheless. After all, friends are to a large degree people with whom we have shared experiences, and whose feelings we understand even without being told.

And finally, as we run, we are able to truly think about our relationship to the ultimate reality of the universe. As we go through life, we get caught up in our daily routines. We have concerns about work or school, plus countless social pressures. When we go home at night, many of us need a little "down" time to relax before going to bed—and so we watch television. Now none of these things are bad in themselves (not even television!), but when they take up absolutely *all* of our time, they can become problematic because they interfere with these three components of a healthy spirituality, especially our relationship with the Divine. So when you go for a run, and I mean a good run of a half-hour or more, you block out a chunk of time when you have the opportunity to meditate on the reality of God.

Your Spiritual Running Journal

Take a moment to think about the specific things that seem to get in the way of having a good relationship with yourself, with others, and with God. Perhaps you would like to go for a run as you think about this, but don't rush yourself in this task. Use the following questions to get you started in writing about this topic in your spiritual journal.

- What is the main thing standing in the way of having a good relationship with yourself (or with others or with God)?
- What caused that obstacle?
- What can you begin to do to dismantle or overcome that obstacle?

Before you next go for a run, review what you've written so you can ponder it as you run and perhaps discover what you can do to remedy your situation.

WHY *NOW*? WHY THE SPIRITUALITY OF *RUNNING*?

Almost a century ago, the great psychoanalyst Sigmund Freud gave a series of lectures on religion that were published under the title *The Future of an Illusion* (1927). In those lectures, he predicted the end of religion because of the growth of science, which he believed would displace religion and the need for such "wish-fulfilling delusions."[8] Nearly forty years later, in 1966, *Time* magazine published what was to become one of its most famous issues. The cover was simple. There were no photographs, or drawings, or clever caricatures. The cover simply posed a question, written in big red letters on a black background: "Is God Dead?"[9] The cover story was about the "death of God" movement, which proclaimed that humanity had "come of age" and that we no longer needed to believe in the outdated remnants of an ancient, prescientific religion.

But science has not made religion obsolete, and the "death of God" movement faded away almost as quickly as it came. Since the 1960s, religion has grown in this country. Recent polls indicate that in the United States more and more people believe in some sort of God. More and more people claim to believe in the tenets of established religion. But it is also interesting to note that fewer people are actually attending churches, synagogues, and other religious places of worship. Ironically, though the number of people having religious beliefs has increased, membership and attendance at traditional religious services has decreased. Put another way, although the prediction of Sigmund Freud has not proved correct, people do seem to be less interested in traditional forms of organized religion.

This observation can be taken even further. Not only are people less interested in traditional organized religion, but many of these people also seem to be creating their own personal religions. In the classic book about individualism in American life, *Habits of the Heart*,[10] sociologist Robert N. Bellah first brought this to the attention of the American public. His conclusions, based on extensive interviews with people from a variety of economic and religious backgrounds, were in some ways shocking, as the following example illustrates. A young nurse named Sheila Larson mused: "I believe in God. I'm not a religious fanatic. I can't remember the last time I went to church. My faith has carried me a long way. It's Sheilaism. Just my own little voice."[11] Clearly, even though many people are dissatisfied with traditional organized religious spirituality, they are still finding their own ways of being spiritual. So what makes running one such way of being spiritual?

Perhaps the most foundational reason is that, of all sports, running is the most natural. Children not only have an inner impulse that spurs them to learn how to walk, but they also have a deeply rooted impulse to run. We can assist them in learning both, but the impulse is already there. This point was brought home to me very powerfully a few years ago. The cross-country team that I help coach was stretching in the lobby of the college gymnasium. On this particular day, a number of parents brought their children for youth hockey practice at the college rink, accompanied by even younger siblings. As the parents were talking together and the older children were getting ready for their practice, the younger children—some three, four, and five years old—were playing together

> "Run the way you remember running in your childhood—loose and carefree. Don't look around and compare your running form with anyone else's."
> —Amby Burfoot, *The Principles of Running: Practical Lessons from My First 100,000 Miles*

by simply running around in the lobby. Seeing this made very clear to me a couple of basic but important points. First, running is fun. For those children (and just about every other child I have ever seen), running is a form of play. And second, running is natural. There are no rules or special equipment. You don't have to be taught how to run—people *just do it*.

Since it seems clear that many people are looking for ways of becoming spiritual or of exploring the spiritual dimension of themselves, and because running is one of the most natural and spontaneous activities we engage in, it could be argued that running can be used as a vehicle for that spiritual quest. But there is more.

THE JOY OF RUNNING

Running is a natural form of *play*, and it is also an excellent vehicle for a spiritual quest because it often produces special feelings of transcendence. The legendary runner Roger Bannister discusses these feelings on one of the opening pages of his autobiography, where he describes a childhood memory of running:

> What are the moments that stand out clearly when we look back on childhood and youth?
>
> I remember a moment when I stood barefoot on firm dry sand by the sea. The air had a special quality as if it had a life of its own. The sound of breakers on the shore shut out all others. I looked up at the clouds, like great white-sailed galleons, chasing proudly inland. I looked down at the regular ripples on the sand, and could not absorb so much beauty. I was taken aback—each of the myriad particles of sand was perfect in its way. I looked more closely, hoping perhaps that my eyes might detect some flaw. But for once there was nothing to detract from all this beauty.
>
> In this supreme moment I leapt in sheer joy. I was startled, and frightened, by the tremendous excitement that so few steps could create. I glanced round uneasily to see if anyone was watching. A few more steps—self-consciously now and firmly gripping the original excitement. The earth seemed almost to move with me. I was running now, and a fresh rhythm entered my body. No longer conscious of my movement I discovered a new unity with nature. I had found a new source of power and beauty, a source I never dreamt existed.[12]

In these few sentences, Bannister identifies a number of feelings—joy, excitement, and a sense of unity with nature, as well as being a source of power and beauty. And he associates all these feelings with his early experience of running. These, and many other feelings, are intimately related to what I am calling here the spirituality of running. I suspect that the joy and other feelings he speaks of are not merely a degree of happiness, but are much closer to what Oxford professor C. S. Lewis, author of *The Chronicles of Narnia*, described as Joy (with a capital J) in his spiritual autobiography *Surprised by Joy*. There, Lewis wrote that "Joy itself, considered simply as an event in my own mind, turned out to be of no value at all. All the value lay in that of which Joy was the desiring. And that object, quite clearly, was no state of my own mind or body at all."[13]

> "There's no reason to do any of it—to run, walk, or race—unless it brings joy into your life. You can find satisfaction in the act of moving your body from the first tentative steps. There's no need to postpone the joy until you've reached a dreamt up point of experience or skill. As a beginner, the time to find and embrace the joy is now."
> —John Bingham,[14] *No Need for Speed*

This takes me to my second point. What that object is—the object of Joy that Lewis speaks of, and I believe it is also the source and object of the joy and excitement of which Roger Bannister speaks—is the Sacred or, quite simply, God. And running helps us experience that.

THE FIVE STAGES OF A RUNNER

Most likely you do not have an experience of God every time you run, at least not in the way most people would think of it. And there are good reasons for that. For example, a lot of people I talk to who run regularly confess that they don't actually *like* running. They only do it as a form of exercise and do not really enjoy it. Many people actually cite this as the biggest reason why they listen to music while they run—it takes their mind off of the pain, discomfort, and boredom of running. Similarly, a lot of people have been conditioned to regard running as a form of punishment, which is likely a result of participation in high school sports or a gym class. This common dislike of running has prompted the now-famous message emblazoned on the T-shirts of cross-country runners across the nation: "My sport is your sport's punishment!"

For these and other reasons, many people, when they are running, are not even open to the possibility of experiencing anything more than feeling tired, being out of breath, and having sore muscles, while, hopefully, burning calories. But what are the conditions that are most conducive to spiritual running? Former Olympic distance runner Jeff Galloway has written a great training manual for runners called *Galloway's Book on Running*. His book has a really interesting chapter called "The Five Stages of a Runner," which can help us sort out some answers to this question.[15] In what follows, I will summarize his main points.

The first stage of running identified by Galloway is appropriately called "The Beginner." Beginnings are often difficult anyway, and when one begins something physically strenuous like running, the difficulties cannot be overestimated. One of the common characteristics of people at this level is self-consciousness. They worry about what they look like and what other people might think of them. Consequently, they are very hesitant to run anywhere people can see them. The beginning runner is also beset by many distractions, criticisms, and temptations to stop. These temptations can come from friends who make fun of a new runner, or they can come from inside the runner. It is easy for the beginner to skip a workout because he or she wants to sleep in, or because something else appears more attractive. Thus, for the beginner who is not used to running, progress may be much slower than expected. And in a society like ours where everyone looks for quick results, the beginner may be especially tempted to quit. Discouragement and failure are not uncommon at this stage.

But for the person who sticks with it, he or she eventually reaches Galloway's second stage of running, which is that of

"The Jogger." Many definitions of jogging attempt to set it apart from running. Although these definitions may serve a purpose for the people who make them, in the end there is very little value in making the distinction. That is why my favorite definition is the one given by George Sheehan: "The difference between a jogger and a runner is a race entry blank."

For Galloway, the jogger is a person who has moved beyond the beginning stage and has become more used to running. The jogger tends to enjoy running more than the beginner and may even look forward to the daily run. Also, at the end of a run, the jogger often experiences a psychological and physical feeling of well-being, what Galloway calls a "glow." Although an injury can take the jogger out of running for a while and put the jogger back in the beginner stage while he or she recovers, the jogger is more at home with running than the beginner is. It is interesting that although a beginner often experiences boredom while running, joggers usually become less bored with running as the distance they are able to run increases.

The third stage is "The Competitor." The main mark of this stage is a high interest—even an obsession—with competition. The competitive drive grows in a person until he or she no longer values the daily run for its own worth, but thinks of a run simply as a stepping-stone toward improving performance at races. Some good lessons are learned in this stage. Thus, for many competitors, their achievements in running show them what they might be able to do in other areas of their life, and the struggle of competition can help them discover a lot about themselves. But often they go through some pretty extreme circumstances to learn them.

The fourth stage identified by Galloway is "The Athlete." For a person at this stage, running is a means of personal expression almost like a work of art. The athlete does not measure success in terms of minutes and seconds, as the competitor does. Rather, success is judged by the athlete him- or herself and is based on the quality of the effort.

The final stage of running Galloway calls "The Runner." In this stage the best elements of the other four stages are combined. Although the runner is dedicated to the sport, the primary focus of life is not running. There is a balance of fitness, competition, and training, which are blended into the runner's *whole life*. According to Galloway, the runner can "appreciate the peace and inner reflection provided by the solitary run" more than he or she could in the other stages. Above all, he says, "the joy lies not in the race, but *in the running*" [italics mine].

THE FIVE STAGES AND SPIRITUALITY

Understanding that runners often go through distinct stages in their running helps us understand why some runners are more likely to have a spiritual experience on their runs. But which stages will be most conducive to spirituality? That's not easy to say in advance because I am sure that individual differences will have an effect on this. I very strongly believe that spirituality *can* be experienced on all levels, but certain stages may be more conducive to spirituality than others.

The beginner is easily distracted by the discomfort and boredom of running and is self-conscious, worrying about what he or she looks like to others. But if beginners can consciously make an effort to divert their attention away from such things, they will not only be more likely to make faster progress as a runner, but will be more open to the spiritual benefits as well. The jogger is one who is at home with running, enjoys it, and can easily make the transition to spiritual running. It is when we come to the competitor that a potentially dangerous obsession with competition can take attention away from spirituality. The competitor measures self-worth with personal accomplishment at races, rank in age groups, and the achievement of better and better times. As long as competitors can put their running into a proper perspective, enjoying accomplishments but not defining themselves in terms of race results, they too can find the spiritual side of running. With the athlete and the runner, the dangers of competition are for the most part behind them. Their running has a more positive and balanced place in their lives, which puts them in a good position to experience the spiritual aspects of the sport.

IT IS REALLY VERY SIMPLE

An interesting thing happened last fall after I had just finished a six-mile run with the cross-country team and was walking into the gym at the college where I teach. I was all sweaty and probably looked very, *very* tired, and as I approached the water fountain for a much-needed drink, a couple of the college basketball players called over to me. They had just enrolled in the course I was teaching, "The Spirituality of Running," and with a laugh, they asked if I had had a spiritual experience on my run that day. Although they meant it as a joke, I was able to truthfully say to them that yes, I had.

Having a spiritual experience doesn't mean that I have visions of Jesus while I am on my morning run. It doesn't mean that I hear voices from beyond the grave or that I occasionally encounter burning bushes the way Moses did more than three thousand years ago. Spirituality can mean as little as an appreciation of the beauty of God's creation or the enjoyment of the gift of friendship. Spirituality can also mean much more—and the activity of running *can* make a big contribution to that experience, but this leads me to the next chapter.

Your Spiritual Running Journal

Before you go on to the next chapter, take some time to think about the following questions and write about them in your journal.

- Are you like the young nurse who made her own religion of "Sheilaism," or do you believe in a traditional religion?
- What do you consider to be the ultimate reality (God or something else)?

- Have you ever felt the joy and excitement in running like what Roger Bannister wrote about? If so, describe the event as best as you can.
- Have you ever felt the Joy that C. S. Lewis wrote about? When did it happen? Were other people there or were you alone? What might have caused it?
- Which of the five stages of a runner best describes you? Are you satisfied with being in that stage, or would you like to progress to another stage? What will you have to do to get there?

On Your Next Run

The next time you go for a run, let yourself warm up to the idea that you're not merely going for an everyday run, but that this can now become a spiritual practice in your life—a means by which you can establish a healthy relationship with yourself, with others, and with the Divine. Don't try to accomplish too much during a single run. Instead, let yourself explore this notion by pondering what you've written in your spiritual running journal. At which of the five stages of a runner are you currently running? Is it the most conducive for a spiritual practice? If not, would temporarily easing back from a focus on competition, or perhaps working to advance from the beginning stages, help? Whatever you decide, remember that this is your own personal practice. Let it be the joy that running can be.

● ● ● ●

CHAPTER TWO

WHAT IS SPIRITUALITY?

There are more things in heaven and earth, Horatio,
Than are dreamt of in your philosophy.

—Hamlet, *Act I, Scene V*

The simple believes everything,
But the prudent looks where he is going.

—*Proverbs 14:15*

For many people, the mention of a spiritual experience brings to mind very specific and often dramatic events, like the following two episodes:

- Early in the first century, after Jesus was crucified by the Romans, a rabbi named Saul—later known to Christians as St. Paul—traveled to the city of Damascus. On his way there, he was blinded by a great light, which caused him to fall to the ground. As he lay stunned, he heard the voice of Jesus, who spoke to him from heaven.[1]

- In the early seventh century, when he was about forty years old, Muhammad spent time by himself in the hill country outside Mecca practicing the spiritual exercises called *tahannuth.* As a consequence, Muhammad had a series of experiences, which he later described as visions of an angel who spoke to him.[2]

While I don't deny that such experiences may be possible for some people (and the history of the world's religions is full of stories of people who make such claims), that is *not* what I am proposing the spirituality of running primarily has to offer. Spiritual experiences are far more common than those dramatic events and are usually something much more down-to-earth. The enjoyment of a sunrise can be a spiritual experience, as can the experience of friendship. The feeling of comfort in time of need or sorrow, as well as contentment with yourself, are all within the range of spiritual experiences.

I recently attended a lecture by an artist friend of mine. During his lecture, he showed images of art through history to illustrate his talk. At one point, he showed an early medieval picture of Mary and the child Jesus and told his audience that he had seen this image many times reproduced in books, but when he saw the actual picture in a church while on a trip to Italy he was brought to tears. This, too, I would say, was a spiritual experience, even though my artist friend is not a traditionally religious man.

So if spirituality can be as simple as the appreciation of beauty and friendship, many people have experienced the spirituality of running without even knowing it. The spirituality I am talking about is *at least* that, but can be much more, and it will be our task to explore some of the ways in which we can enhance our spiritual experience of running.

Is There a Spiritual World?

Although there is a growing thirst for religion (even nontraditional religion) in our society, secularism, or antireligious sentiment, has also been growing. Even though many people in our society are religious, a lot of people are not. And even religious people are often skeptical when it comes to talking about the spiritual side of the universe. But is there more to the world than meets the eye?

A common answer to this question is no. Such people believe that reality is only what we can see with our eyes, feel with our hands, hear with our ears, or smell and taste. If something can't be experienced with our five senses, it is at best a product of our minds or imagination. People who believe this are called *reductionists*.[3] They think that the universe is totally reducible to the physical substances that make it up. For a reductionist, a human being is composed of chemicals joined together in a particular way to produce a human person. For a reductionist, the human brain is nothing but a biological organ connected to various parts of the body by nerves. What we call "thought" and "mind" are just names for the functions of the brain, functions produced by a series of electrochemical impulses in the nervous system. If that is true, consciousness is nothing but a product of these biochemical processes. This whole reductionist idea has led some people to put a value on the human body based solely on the cost of the substances that make it up. When I was a boy in school, we were told in science class that the human body, when analysed as a collection of chemicals, was worth about 99 cents! These days the human body has gone up to about $4.50 (inflation!).

But I don't think the reductionist is right, and a lot of scientists (and other people) would agree with me. A human being is far more than the sum of his or her parts, more than just a bunch of chemicals that are able to function in a certain way. And this has implications for a lot of things.

If the reductionist *were* correct, a painting would be no more than bits of paint, of a specific chemical composition, applied to a canvas to reflect light in a certain way, which we are able to receive through the receptors on our faces (our eyes) and which produce reactions in our brain, and so on. But I disagree. I think there is much more at work—there is beauty, which cannot be reduced to the sum of the physical parts of a painting.

Also, if the reductionist *were* correct, love would be nothing more than a psychosexual response of one member of our species to another, with the accompanying instincts for protection of the mate. Again, I think there is more at work. I love my wife, which means that we have a connection on a deeper level than just the biological. When people talk of soul mates, I believe that really *does* mean something.

If the reductionist were correct, ethics and morality would be nothing more than pragmatic rules. The reductionist might say that since we can't get away with being totally selfish in our actions at all times, we give a little in order to get something. The result of this kind of thinking, they say, is the system of right and wrong that we experience in our society. Other societies might have different rules, and we happen to have the rules we do because our society has settled on them as the best compromise in the effort to keep the members of society from killing each other.

Finally, according to the reductionist, the human being is just a biological entity comprised of organs performing their various functions, the brain being nothing but another biological organ. But just as there is more to a work of art than specks of paint on a canvas, more to love than a biological activity, and more to morality than social contracts, there is more to a human being than his or her physical body. There is in all of these areas an element that we call the spiritual. And it is in all these areas that we can discuss what I have called the spirituality of running.

If the reductionists *were* correct, running would simply be a physical activity. According to biologists, thousands—even millions—of years of human evolution has produced in us the desire to run.[4] These biologists believe that evolution has programmed us as a species to run because our ancestors often needed to run to catch food or avoid danger. For biologists, early humans were like the animals in the following quotation by an anonymous runner: "Every morning in Africa, an antelope wakes up. It knows it must outrun the fastest lion, or it will be killed. Every morning in Africa, a lion wakes up. It knows it must run faster than the antelope, or it will starve. It doesn't matter whether you're a lion or an antelope—when the sun comes up, you'd better be running." Thus, according to some of these evolutionary biologists, the glow that many runners experience after a nice long run is merely a remnant of a biological response our ancestors developed to the pain they experienced—kind of like a reward that the body was giving them—while running after food or from danger. For the reductionists, running is just this physical activity *and nothing more*.

Yet the world is more than just what we can see. Beauty, love, good, and bad are all real. And most important, there is something more to us as human beings. We're not *just* animals. So when we run and do other activities, if we experience something of beauty, if we experience love (or at least friendship), and if we encounter other people, there is always more than meets the eye—there is a spiritual dimension.

You don't have to be a religious person to experience this spiritual dimension when running. But for most people, spirituality *is* closely related to religion or belief in God.

Is There a God?

Is there more to the universe than we can see? Is there a God? Sociologist Peter L. Berger has written a very interesting book called *A Rumor of Angels: Modern Society and the Rediscovery of the Supernatural*,[5] in which he discusses the fact that there are in the world what he calls "signals of transcendence." By this, he means that there are certain experiences common to all of us that appear to point beyond those experiences to something transcendent. This is also what C. S. Lewis was speaking of when he wrote, "If I find in myself a desire that no experience in this world can satisfy, the most probable explanation is that I was made for another world."[6]

These observations by Berger and Lewis assist us in the attempt to find spiritual elements in running by showing that there are

indicators of the Divine all around us in everyday experiences. God
tends to work in small, consistent ways and not just in miracles.

WHAT IS SPIRITUALITY?

There has been a lot of talk recently about spirituality.[7] But what
does the word mean? For some people, the word is a synonym
for religion itself. It seems to be fashionable these days to talk not
about a particular religion like Christianity or Judaism but about
"spirituality," as if that word includes all the best that a religion
can offer but avoids the unwanted or unnecessary specifics of a
particular religion. The word *spirituality* is sometimes used to
describe religious ideas not associated with the particular biases
of specific organized religious traditions. Consequently, *spirituality* has become a word with very little content—it is just a vague
word that gives the appearance of being meaningful or even profound, but doesn't really stand for anything in particular.

Part of the problem is that even specialists in the study of
religion have a hard time defining this term. So when I use the
word *spirituality* in this book I would like to give it a very specific
meaning. To do this, it might be helpful to think in a general way
about religions. All religions have three basic elements. The first
element is theology, or the beliefs of any given religion. Although
religions differ as to *what* they believe, all religions *have* religious
beliefs. Some religions believe that there is one God; they are
called monotheistic. Some religions believe that there are many
gods; they are called polytheistic. Christians have some very specific beliefs about the man called Jesus of Nazareth that are not
shared by the members of other religions, just as Muslims
have some specific beliefs about the Prophet Muhammad that are
not shared by the members of other religions.

The second element of all religions is that they all have a set
of values. These values can sometimes be expressed in a set of
rules, but they usually go far beyond a simple set of rules. These
values are specific ideas about what is good and what is bad in the

moral sense, and within individual religions, they have a claim on believers' lives.

The third element of religion is its way of life. Being a member of a religion is not just about believing certain things and holding a certain consistent set of values (although it is partly about that). The way you live your life in light of your beliefs and values is what I call spirituality in a general sense. This may include going to church, synagogue, or temple. It may also include daily acts of devotion, such as prayer before meals and before going to bed, reading the scriptures, studying the meaning of scriptures, and allowing the values implicit in and taught by your religion to become a part of your everyday life. It can also include sensing the presence of God, or the gods, or whatever you believe the sacred reality to be. I think the seventeenth-century Carmelite Brother Lawrence expressed this well when he wrote the following, referring to his specifically Christian understanding of the Holy: "That practice which is alike the most holy, the most general, and the most needful in the spiritual life is the practice of the presence of God."[8]

That is spirituality.

Your Spiritual Running Journal

Before reading any further in this chapter, pause for a while to think about the following questions and write about them in your journal.

- Have you ever had a spiritual experience?
- Have you had a spiritual experience while running?

To help you write your answers to these questions, the following guidelines may be helpful:

1. Choose a significant event from your experience of running. The experience can be positive or negative, and the fact that you remember this event at all means that it is significant to you.

2. Describe the event in detail. Use the following points to help in writing about the event. Who was there? What was going on? Where and when did this event take place? Include details of what you saw, heard, and felt. What time of year was it? How was the weather? What was the time of day?

3. In light of our discussion of spirituality, what spiritual elements were present in this experience? Spiritual elements include such things as friendship, love, love of self (in the good sense!), appreciation of beauty (various sorts of beauty), and even—yes, you guessed it—a sense of the presence of God.

4. Include a section on how writing about this event made you feel. You might find it helpful to answer the following questions: Is that feeling different from what you felt when you had the original experience? What questions are now raised by writing about the experience? Why did you choose to write about this experience?

RELIGION AND RUNNING IN HISTORY

But the question remains: why is running a powerful instrument of spirituality? There is no simple answer to this. Running has been an activity of necessity and enjoyment for thousands of years, and in a number of cultures, running has had a close association with spirituality and religion. Several striking examples come to mind.

In ancient Greece, the Olympic Games were actually religious festivals. Although no one knows exactly when they began, we know that there were already Olympic Games by the year 776 BCE. The first Olympic events were all related to running. At Olympia, the site of the ancient Games, the track (*stadion*) was 192 meters long. It was not a nice oval shape like modern tracks, but was straight with a hairpin turn at each end. The competitors had to run the length of the track, around a pillar, and back to the starting point, where there was another pillar. The longer races required several of these "laps." The shortest of the running events in the ancient Olympics was a sprint called the *stade* in which competitors ran one length of the track. The *diaulos* was a race of two lengths, down and back. The longest race was called "the long one" (*dolichos*), which was not a standard distance; it could include up to twenty-four laps, a distance similar to the modern 5,000-meter run.[9]

The religious nature of these games was natural and logical. Ancient Greek religion was polytheistic, and the gods themselves were conceived in anthropomorphic terms. They were understood to be physical beings shaped just like humans—only bigger, more beautiful (or handsome), more muscular, and, perhaps most important, immortal. According to Greek myth, the gods were also capable of making love to mortal humans, which sometimes resulted in offspring—the demigods (such as Hercules).[10] Since the gods were physical beings like humans, the humans who were closest in physical form to the gods were the Olympic champions. But this all came to an end in the year 393 CE, when the Christian emperor Theodocius I (379–395) abolished the Olympic Games, not because the games unduly emphasized the body but because they were Pagan festivals. Theodocius felt that the religious basis of the games was incompatible with Christianity.[11]

Another connection between running and religion comes from Japan. On Mount Hiei near Kyoto lives a group of Buddhist monks belonging to the Tendai sect. These monks are more popularly known as the "Marathon Monks" because of the amazing distances they are reputed to cover in relatively short periods of time.[12] According to accounts available here in the West, these monks undertake a thousand-day physical challenge, which makes the 2006 endurance feat of ultramarathoner Dean Karnazes, in which he ran fifty marathons in fifty consecutive days, look tame.[13]

Since 1885, only about forty-eight men have actually completed this seven-year challenge, and those who have are called *dai-ajari*, or "great master." The most recent person to become a great master was Genshin Fujinami, who achieved this goal in 2003. It is not surprising that so few are reported to have completed this feat. First, the extreme nature of the challenge is surely discouraging to many, and second, those who attempt it are expected to commit suicide if they are not successful. The nature of the challenge is as follows. Each of the first three years includes 100 consecutive days in which the monks reputedly run about 40 kilometers (25 miles) per day. The number of consecutive days of running 40 kilometers is increased to 200 in the forth and fifth years. In the final two years, the monks step up their pace. During the sixth year, these Marathon Monks run around 60 kilometers (37.5 miles) per day for 100 consecutive days, and in the seventh year they run 84 kilometers (52.5 miles) each day for 100 consecutive days.

According to John Stevens, who has written about these monks, they begin their run while it is still nighttime, running over uneven mountain paths, during all sorts of weather, including rain and low temperatures. Further, they do not have the advantages of modern footwear—they run in straw sandals. During the days of running, their diet includes vegetables, potatoes, noodles, tofu, and miso soup.

A final example of the religious use of running is the Lung-gom-pa runners of Tibet. Far less is known of this mysterious running sect than of the Marathon Monks of Japan. According to some, these runners appear to fly when they run, sometimes covering more than 300 kilometers (200 miles) in a day, and even running for as much as forty-eight hours nonstop. One of the only accounts of Lung-gom-pa runners is from the French explorer Alexandra David-Néel in *Magic and Mystery in Tibet*.[14] In a now-famous passage from that book, David-Néel recounts her first encounter with one of these runners in 1924. While traveling in a grassy region in northern Tibet, a Lung-gom-pa runner was spotted in the distance. At first they thought him to be a lost traveler, but as they got closer, they realized that he was moving at an amazingly high speed. At first, David-Néel wanted to talk with him, but was warned against doing so because, as she was told, the god that lives within him would then escape and the runner would surely die. Respectful of their beliefs, she satisfied herself with observing the lone runner and later wrote the following description of him:

> I could clearly see his perfectly calm impassive face and wide-open eyes with their gaze fixed on some invisible far-distant object situated somewhere high up in space. The man did not run. He seemed to lift himself from the ground, proceeding by leaps. It looked as if he had been endowed with the elasticity of a ball and rebounded each time his feet touched the ground. His steps had the regularity of a pendulum.[15]

WHAT RELEVANCE ARE THESE EXAMPLES TO YOU AND ME?

This discussion of ancient Greece, the Tendai monks of Japan, and Buddhist monks in Tibet is very interesting, but what value is all of that to you and me? I don't believe in physical gods who live on the top of Mount Olympus, and I don't believe that as athletes we are attempting to become godlike either, so my motivation for running is different from that of the ancient Greeks. My beliefs as a monotheist and a Christian are different from the Buddhist monks of Japan and Tibet, so I, myself, gain very little spiritual motivation from the Marathon Monks or the Lung-gom-pa runners. And even if I shared their beliefs, I could never duplicate those amazing feats of physical endurance. Perhaps your own motivations and beliefs also differ from those of the Greeks, Marathon Monks, and Lung-gom-pa runners. So what lessons are there to be learned from these runners?

You can see in these examples that there is a clear and natural connection between spirituality and running that has been recognized and practiced for millennia. That is, running itself is a mode for spiritual growth that other sports may not be. Recently I was in a conversation with a man who, when he heard that I was teaching a course on the spirituality of running, spoke of a friend of his who was interested in the spirituality of fly-fishing. I tried to communicate to him that it is not the same thing. Although we can be spiritual in everything we do in our daily lives, there is something special about the activity of running that sets it apart from most other human activities.

> "Shoes are your most important purchase. If there's one place not to scrimp, this is it.... Which type of shoe you need depends on your feet and your body. If you're a big person, you'll probably need greater-than-average cushion. If your feet tend to roll inward or outward with each step, you'll need a stable 'motion control' shoe."
>
> —Alberto Salazar,[16] *Alberto Salazar's Guide to Running: A Champion's Revolutionary Program to Revitalize Your Fitness*

For example, running, unlike many other sports or human activities, doesn't need external tools or devices: you have your body, and that's all you need. In other words, there is minimal "stuff" to get in the way of running (equipment breaking down, for example). In the ancient Olympic Games, the athletes competed naked. Although in the modern world runners wear clothes—shorts, shirt, and shoes—they don't *need* them for the activity itself. The clothes are additions that protect runners from the weather and the terrain and are generally minimal: the shirts are small and light, the shorts are lightweight, and the shoes, which give added support to the feet, are also light and comfortable. Running encourages *simplicity*—a principle that tends to foster spiritual growth.

This, in turn, helps you experience a feeling of *freedom* and *joy* when you run, a feeling that is different from anything you experience through any other purely human activity. Moreover, when you allow your run to be a spiritual experience, you participate in an ancient tradition that gives your practice a certain *gravitas*. The sacred art of running is not some newfangled theory: this approach to spirituality has been practiced and proven for millennia in cultures that have spanned the globe. You are in good company!

Your Spiritual Running Journal

Before you go on to the next chapter, take some time to think about the following questions and write about them in your journal.

- Have you had any spiritual experiences in your life? If so, were they dramatic or more subtle? Do you want to have more or different kinds of spiritual experiences?
- In your everyday life, do you tend to view things as a reductionist would, as merely a thing or an object? Or is finding the meaning behind the material world a natural activity for you?
- Have you ever experienced a "signal of transcendence"—a thing or event that seemed to glow with a presence of the Divine?
- Until you read this chapter, how did you define spirituality? Was that similar to how we are working with that word in this book?

On Your Next Run

The next time you go for a run, spend a portion of your time thinking about the spiritual and religious practices you have used in your life. What practices were useful to you? What made them helpful and meaningful? Most of us have tried spiritual disciplines that for one reason or another didn't work for us. What kinds of practices were a waste of time for you? What has drawn you to explore running as a form of spirituality? Can you see yourself practicing this for years and decades to come?

● ● ● ●

CHAPTER THREE

SEEING GOD
WHILE RUNNING

I don't see any God up here.
—Yuri Gagarin[1]

On April 12, 1961, Yuri Gagarin of the Soviet Union became the first human being to go into outer space and orbit Earth. News media from around the world reported that he made the comment, which appears at the head of this chapter: "I don't see any God up here." This comment came from a citizen of the Soviet Union, which was an explicitly atheist society, so nobody was really surprised by it, even when they disagreed with it. But could anyone really expect him to *see* God up there? Did the fact that he could not see God really mean anything? What would God look like, anyway?

LOOKING AT THE SUN

To suggest an answer to these questions, let me share with you a story about the Roman emperor Hadrian (76–138 CE), who, according to tradition, once visited Rabbi Joshua ben Hananiah. The emperor was fascinated by the Jewish religion and its monotheistic belief. He said to Joshua, "I desire greatly to see your God." So the rabbi took the emperor outside and told him to look directly at the midday sun. "I cannot," said the emperor.

To this the rabbi said, "If you cannot look at the sun, which God created, how much less can you behold the glory of God himself!"[2]

This story makes an important point about the nature of God. It seems to me that the rabbi was trying to tell the emperor that although we cannot look straight at the sun, we do know a lot about the sun, which we can learn in a variety of ways. So, for example, because we can feel the warmth of the sun and look at the way it sheds its light on Earth, we can know that it exists and something of what it is like. We are in the same position with regard to our knowledge of God. Even though we don't see or experience God directly, we can know a lot about God from the world around us. There are reasons to believe that a sacred reality like God exists, and there are also ways to know something of what that sacred reality is like.

SEEING

When you go out for a run, what do you *see* along your favorite route? That may seem like a pretty straightforward question, and you might be imagining the road or trail, the trees or buildings, or the clouds in the sky.

But the question goes deeper than that because the word *see* can be used in at least two ways. First there is the normal way we see: I see with my eyes, and I happen to wear glasses, which correct my vision. When I run, I consciously try to look at things— I mean really *look* at things. I look at the sky. Is it blue and clear? Or are there clouds? I make a conscious effort to look around me as well, to see my immediate surroundings. Are there other people or animals nearby? What about plants? And more than just for safety reasons I take note of the road or trail. Is it smooth or rough? Are there any obstacles?

To really *see* the details of your surroundings on a run is important. Not only does it make the run safer, but it can also help make it more fun. Especially if you are a beginner or somebody who really doesn't like to run, it helps take your mind off the discomfort you may be feeling. And looking around as you run and really *seeing* your surroundings can and should contribute to the spiritual experience. I don't mean that you have to move your head around to look at things all around you (especially when you are on an off-road trail). You shouldn't do anything that will take your mind off where you are going. So while running carefully, all the while looking where you are going, you can also be aware of your surroundings in the ways I have described above.

The cross-country team I help coach sometimes practices at Half-Mile Hill, which has a path winding through grassy fields and is crested by woods. From the top, we can see woods spreading out below us around a large lake and the lovely homes of the local towns nestled among the trees. Particularly in the autumn, the view from the top is beautiful with all the New England fall colors (that is one of the reasons why I love cross-country—it is a fall sport).

During these practices, the team runs up and down the path on that hill as many as eight times. I am always surprised that so many of the athletes don't bother to look at the beautiful view when they reach the top before they make the turn to jog back down the hill. We can see that with our eyes—if we are looking. I always encourage people to see as much as possible when they run.

That is the first sense of the word *see*. But can we see anything more than our surroundings when we run? I think we can.

> "Whenever I travel, I head out for a run at the first available opportunity to get a sense of where I am. Nothing comes close to running for making me feel quickly familiar with a strange place. I have seen some of the most incredible sights—Paris at night, Florence early in the morning, and dusty farm roads in central Illinois just before a thunder storm—that tourists and couch potatoes never see."
>
> —Kathrine Switzer,[3] *Running and Walking for Women Over 40*

SEEING AS

There is a second sense of the word *see*. When we see things with our eyes, our brains also *interpret* what we see. We don't normally think about this; it happens instantly and automatically. You may have heard it said of someone who always has a positive view of things that he or she is "looking at the world through rose-colored glasses." That person may have the same experiences as everyone else, but he or she interprets them in a positive way.

Another example of how the brain interprets what we see is Magic Eye pictures. These puzzles, made up of lots of dots on a page, may seem random at first, but if you look at them in a certain way or from a particular angle, the dots merge to form a three-dimensional image. Similarly, there is the famous duck-rabbit picture, which you can see either as a duck facing one way, or as a rabbit facing the other (see below).

Thus, what we are *looking at* is not always exactly the same as what we *see*. And it varies from person to person. One person

will only see dots of color on a page, but another will see the 3-D image of a human face. One person will see the duck, another person, the rabbit. In both cases, different people are looking at the same marks on the page but are seeing them in significantly different ways. In the mid-twentieth century, Austrian philosopher Ludwig Wittgenstein spoke of this experience in terms of "seeing as."[4] You see something *as* your mind interprets it. You see an illustration in a magazine *as* a collection of random dots or *as* a picture of a human face, the picture *as* a duck or *as* a rabbit. And the sudden recognition of the dots as a face or the lines as a duck (or a rabbit) can be one of those experiences that suddenly hits you like, "Aha! *Now* I see it!"

These "aha" experiences are not limited to seeing with our eyes. We can extend the notion of "seeing as" to include other kinds of experiences—we can speak of "experiencing as." Sometimes a gesture that has no special meaning in itself can take on significance in a particular context. Buying a pizza is not a particularly meaningful activity, but for two people who have had a big argument, the fact that one of them buys a pizza to share might carry with it great significance for the other person and indicate that he or she is no longer angry.

We don't all experience things the same way. If two people go out for a run together, one person may say she had a spiritual experience while the other person may not. As far as their physical senses are concerned, the two people both saw and experienced pretty much the same things. But there is more going on than just seeing with our eyes.

SEEING GOD IS LIKE SEEING AN ARTIST

The relation of an artist to his or her work provides an analogy to the relationship of God to the world. The artist is more than his or her work of art, for the artist created it. But the artist is bound to the work, having poured something of him- or herself into it so that through the work we can know something about the artist.

My wife is an art historian, and sometimes we go to museums together. I remember one occasion when we went to the Museum of Fine Arts in Boston. We were walking around the museum from room to room, and as we entered one room, my wife commented on a particular painting. Just by looking at the picture, she was able to identify the artist, and she was able to tell me a number of things about him. She was able to do this because the artist invested himself in the work of art, and by looking at the picture she was able to recognize aspects of the artist. But there are people who walk from room to room, gazing wearily and uncomprehendingly at the paintings, only knowing that it is "good" for them, as a well-rounded person, to look at artwork. Although they are in the museum, going through the motions, they are not really looking at the art.

We can't see God directly in the trees, mountains, lakes, buildings, and cars. But if we know how to look, we can see God *in* them, because God is present in them. Just about everything has the potential to become a means for seeing God.

WHAT DO YOU SEE WHEN YOU GO FOR A RUN?

When you go for a run, what do you see or experience in the second sense of the word *see*? That may still seem like an unusual question to ask, and it may take some time and some hard thinking on several long runs to be able to answer it. But depending on the beliefs you have accumulated over your lifetime and education, you may have "seen" or "recognized" God on your run.

A lot depends on the context in which we see things. Before introducing the picture of the duck-rabbit earlier in this chapter, if I had told you that I was going to show you a picture of a rabbit, you would not have seen a duck. You often see what you *expect* to see.

That's the way it often is with God and the world, too. Your preconceptions of God or the Sacred will influence how easily you "see" God or the Sacred and, indeed, even influence *what* you see. Just like the optimist who "sees the world through rose-colored glasses," we see the world through Christian glasses or Jewish glasses or Buddhist glasses or still-seeking glasses or even not-sure-what-but-I-believe-*something's*-out-there glasses!

Your Spiritual Running Journal

Take a few minutes to think about what kind of glasses you wear. Again, you can do this on a run or by yourself in a room, but think about it seriously and take your time as you try to answer the following questions.

- What are your beliefs regarding God or some other sacred reality? Do you believe in one God (like Jews, Christians, and Muslims), or do you believe in something else? Why?
- Is this the conception you were raised with? If so, have you ever entertained other ideas about God? If it's not the same, what brought you to a new understanding of the Holy?
- How would you describe God or the Sacred?

MULTITASKING ON THE RUN

These days people commonly multitask—do (or attempt to do) a number of things at once. To practice the spirituality of running also requires a certain amount of multitasking while you run. There are at least three things that you have to do. First, you should always *be careful* and follow all the commonsense advice for runners (don't run in dangerous parts of a city; women shouldn't run alone at night; be careful of cars while running). Second, *look* at your surroundings. Try to really *see* where you are running and the details of your route. Third, *contemplate* your notion of the Sacred. This last point involves thinking about what you wrote in your journal concerning the "glasses" you wear. With practice, this can be a very rewarding spiritual experience and is what I call *contemplative running*.

THE CONTEMPLATIVE RUNNER

It may be helpful to clarify the concept of contemplation a bit more. As I am using the term here, contemplation is the activity of self-consciously living in the presence of what you believe to be the highest reality—for me, that is God. The Trappist monk and spiritual writer Thomas Merton expressed this understanding of contemplation beautifully in the following words:

> Contemplation ... is spontaneous awe at the sacredness of life, of being. It is gratitude for life, for awareness and for being. It is a vivid realization of the fact that life and being in us proceed from an invisible, transcendent and infinitely abundant Source. Contemplation is, above all, awareness of the reality of that Source. It *knows* the Source, obscurely, inexplicably, but with a certitude that goes both beyond reason and beyond simple faith.[5]

And this is what each one of us should strive for when we go out for a contemplative run.

THE GLASSES WE WEAR MAKE A DIFFERENCE

With this in mind, let's return to a discussion of God to find out more about what we may be seeing or experiencing on some of our long runs. Belief in God, or some sort of a sacred reality, is something found in all cultures around the world and at all times in human history. Even though we can't prove the existence of God, the existence of God is one of the most important questions we can ponder because it relates to the ultimate questions of "life, the universe, and everything," to quote from *The Hitchhiker's Guide to the Galaxy*.

When you run, you really come into contact with the world around you and with yourself. When you run, you really open yourself up to seeing and experiencing some pretty interesting things. You see your environment, that is, the world around you wherever it is that you choose to run. You often see other people. And through all of this, you get an opportunity to really see and experience yourself in ways that you normally are not able to. In the context of your beliefs about what is ultimately real, the Sacred, or God, you can "see" and "experience" much more. You can see and experience God's good creation, which includes your own body. Through contemplative running, you indirectly experience the very heart of God, and you are on the road to becoming a spiritual runner.

"In 1990, the Melpomene Institute for Women's Health Research in St. Paul, Minnesota, surveyed 600 women about why they exercise. Seventeen percent said that exercise helped them realize a positive self-image. A better body image is part of a positive self-image—not just because of the weight control that running provides but because of the fitness, endurance, and strength you gain. You feel proud of a body that can run for 3 miles, 5 miles, 10, 20—farther than most people can even walk."
—Claire Kowalchik,[6] *The Complete Book of Running for Women*

As I end this chapter, I would like to share with you what the famous theologian and mathematician Blaise Pascal had to say about God:

> He so arranges the knowledge of himself that he has given signs of himself, visible to those who seek him, and not to those who do not seek him. There is enough light for those who only desire to see, and enough obscurity for those who have a contrary disposition.[7]

Your Spiritual Running Journal

Before you go on to the next chapter, take some time to think about the following questions and write about them in your journal.

- When you go out for a run, what do you see? What are the actual objects and people that you encounter?
- Now consider how you interpret those things in the sense of "seeing as." How do the things you see point to God or reveal aspects of the Holy? How does that make you feel?
- What are some ways that you can learn to "see as" differently?

On Your Next Run

Before you go for your next run, spend time looking over what you've written in your spiritual running journal regarding your beliefs. What do you believe? Why do you believe it? How does that belief color your world? These are big questions that are not always easy to answer, and the answers you first write down may not be the most accurate.

Allow your run to be an expansive time when you allow your responses to turn over in your mind. What else presents itself? What other, perhaps deeper, reasons do you discover? Deepening or altering your spiritual perspective isn't always easy. What motivates you to seek out this new spiritual practice?

Whatever answers present themselves, don't resist. Sometimes wisdom comes in a flash!

● ● ● ●

CHAPTER FOUR

RUNNING AS SANCTUARY

Running is not a religion, it is a place.
—*George Sheehan*[1]

The late runner, doctor, and philosopher George Sheehan was internationally known for the columns and short articles on running that he wrote during his twenty-five years as a contributing writer and medical editor for *Runner's World* magazine. He also traveled all over the world spreading the gospel of running. In one of his essays, he wrote about a lecture tour that included a trip to Alaska. Upon his arrival in Anchorage, he was asked by a reporter, "Is it true that you have called running a religion?" He had, on occasion, made comments about running and religion. They were sometimes jokes, such as when he repeated a story about a woman who said that her husband "used to be a Methodist, but now he's a runner." But sometimes his comments about running and religion were more serious. His reply to the reporter was brief and to the point, but also a little cryptic. He said, "Running is not a religion, it is a place."

This idea came to him after he read *The Genesee Diary: Report from a Trappist Monastery* by Roman Catholic priest and spiritual writer Henri J. M. Nouwen.[2] In the book, Father Nouwen relates how he had gone to a Trappist monastery to live for seven months because he needed a break from the hectic and demanding schedule of writing and lecturing. After arriving, Father Nouwen was given a variety of daily tasks to help with the upkeep of the monastery. In addition, though, Father Nouwen had time to himself—time to think, read, meditate, and pray. But as he said a number of times and in different ways, "The monastery is not built to solve problems, but to praise the Lord in the midst of them."

At the end of the seven months, when he was preparing to leave, Father Nouwen realized that he hadn't really *fixed* or *changed* anything. He was still the same person with the same responsibilities and problems he had before. This trip to the monastery turned out to be just a pause—a break in the action of his busy life. When he returned to his normal life, things would be once again just as they were before, so he turned to the abbot (the head of the monastery) for advice. "You must put ninety minutes aside every day for prayer," he was told. In this way he could take the monastery with him, so to speak; he could create his own sanctuary in the midst of his everyday life. But this required an intention and commitment to do so. He would have to discipline himself to take time for a dialogue with God and with himself every day. Without this daily renewal, what he had accomplished at the monastery would fade away. Only a return to the monastery every day would save him.

George Sheehan was able to say that running, for him, was like that monastery. It is "a place to commune with God and your-self, a place for psychological renewal." This is a basic principle of the spirituality of running. Running is a place. It is a place you can go to be alone—even when there are other people around. It is a place to think. Running helps you concentrate because it takes you out of the often mind-numbing cycle of the everyday routine of going to work, going home, going to bed, getting up, and going to work. Most important, running is a place that you can go to regardless of where you are. Whether you are on a business trip, on vacation, or visiting family, you can still go for a run. The scenery might change, but when you go for a run, that is your special place. Your run can be your own sanctuary.

RUNNING IN LONDON

One of my former students, an avid runner himself, told me a story of a time when his girlfriend broke up with him while he was studying in London. To deal with the pain of this breakup, he went out for a run through the streets of the city. The only unusual thing about this particular run was that he left the college where he was staying at about two in the morning. Initially, he went for this run to tire himself out so that he could go to sleep. As he ran the four-mile circuit around Regent's Park, he reached a point where, as he put it, "it was almost like my mind was blank just sitting in neutral, while my legs churned along."[3] By the time he completed his run, all his feelings of hurt and anger had disappeared and were replaced by a feeling of calmness. As he later described it,

> On this particular run, I finally received a taste of the true spiritual power of running…. I believe that through running I was able to have a meeting with God, who calmed my aching heart and allowed me to momentarily forget my aching legs…. Though it was never my intention to find God that night or seek his healing, I believe that I experienced it nonetheless during this run.

Running around Regent's Park in London became for him a sanctuary—a place where he could go to deal with his feelings and, as he stated it, feel the presence of God.

In a now-famous passage, philosopher and mathematician Alfred North Whitehead once remarked that religion "is what the individual does with his own solitariness."[4] Years later, the great twentieth-century theologian and Jewish spiritual writer Abraham Joshua Heschel observed that "[r]eligion is not 'what man does with his solitariness.' Religion is what man does with the presence of God. And the spirit of God is present whenever we are willing to accept it."[5] That young man, running by himself in the streets of London, was open to the presence of God on his run. And the activity of running in his time of anger and sadness brought him to his special place, his sanctuary, where he could realize that, in the end, he was not alone. Going to your sanctuary doesn't guarantee an experience of God, but it helps you be open to God.

WHAT IS A SANCTUARY?

Talk of running as a place should remind us that not all places are experienced the same. A simple example is a library, a place where people go to find books and read in silence. It is a separate place, set apart from busy shopping malls and noisy classrooms. When you go into a library, you automatically get quiet and speak in hushed tones. It's the same with a church, a synagogue, and other places of worship—you immediately become quiet when you enter because you know this is a special kind of place. Similarly, the places where we run can become special places for us—even if only for the duration of our run.

> "My dirty running shoes fill me with joy. They've taken me over farm fences in Illinois, through streams in Colorado, rain forests in New Zealand, and on manure-covered bridle paths in England. They are my passports to freedom and my license to revisit my childhood. When I look at my running shoes, I see the steps of my past and the pathway to my future."
> —Kathrine Switzer, *Running and Walking for Women Over 40*

Not only are all places not experienced in the same way, but also *time* is not always experienced the same either. When I am feeling good and am in reasonably good shape, running is easy and my workouts seem to fly by; a sixty-minute workout feels a lot shorter.

And although it is true that "time flies when you're having fun," in difficult situations, time seems to go extra slowly. And I bet most of us have had that unusual feeling when we are on vacation and a day in the middle of the week just *feels* like a Sunday.

Once you recognize that not all times and places are experienced in the same way, you can begin to be intentional about your runs as spiritual events and specifically as your personal sanctuary. First, you have to be careful to pick an appropriate course to run. It is helpful to make it a course that is particularly enjoyable. That doesn't mean that it has to be an easy run; sometimes a difficult course can be enjoyable, too. Most people try to run in a park or in the woods, because the scenery is nice and there are fewer people. Most important, though, you should pick a place that is enjoyable to you.

ROUTINES, TRADITIONS, AND RITUALS

We all have our own way of doing things. When you wake up in the morning, what do you do? Do you make coffee, take a shower, read the newspaper, have a bowl of cereal? Do you do these things the same way and in the same order every day? Often people describe such repeated actions as a morning ritual, but I want to suggest that these are not rituals, but rather routines. These are simply repeated actions, like brushing your teeth, that have no larger significance beyond the actions themselves.

Other types of repeated actions do have special meanings we associate with them. Let's call those actions *traditions*. Every year, we celebrate birthdays, and in our culture, having a cake with candles is a tradition. All over the country, students graduate from high schools and colleges. The commencement exercises are a tradition. Saying "bless you" when someone sneezes is a tradition. But for the most part, these traditions are not particularly religious or spiritual.

Runners also have many traditions. The modern Olympic Games, for example, are full of traditions. Before the games there is the tradition of having runners relay the lighted torch from Athens to the site of the competition. In the track competitions, the winner of a race will take a victory lap. In all events, the national anthem of the gold-medal winner is played. Outside the Olympics, many road races hold a large pasta "carb-loading" meal for the runners the night before the race.

Rituals, though, stand apart from routines and traditions because they carry "an ultimate value, meaning, sacrality, and significance for someone."[6] That is, a ritual is an action that somehow touches the foundations of what that person considers ultimately real and sacred.

One simple ritual, that of making the sign of the cross, comes from the Roman Catholic tradition. For many centuries, people have performed this small ritual. A person takes his or her right hand and brings the tips of the fingers first to the head, then the heart, then the left shoulder, and lastly the right shoulder. This simple gesture traces an invisible cross and signifies both the cross of Jesus Christ and the Holy Trinity (Father, Son, and Holy Spirit).

Since my college days, I have often seen runners cross themselves before a race. For those runners, as long as the gesture is something they take seriously, the race they are about to take part in is no longer just a physical act but is, to a certain extent, a religious or spiritual event.

You probably already run routinely, and you might have even developed some traditions around your running—perhaps you run in a certain 5K race every year. But our runs can also be our sanctuary if we intentionally incorporate ritual into our routine.

MUSIC AND RUNNING

Music performs a number of functions in religious traditions, among them, helping people get into the proper state of mind for worship as well as helping separate regular space from sacred space. As such, we can use music ritualistically to help us establish our sanctuary—our place for finding true spirituality. Robert

Wuthnow, professor of the sociology of religion at Princeton University, stated in a recent interview that music helps him in this very way. Although he has never been good at meditation or spiritual reading, he is finding that music helps.

> Music focuses my attention on God, or puts me in an attitude of worship or devotion, and quiets my thoughts.... It moves me from a place of quiet to a place of exaltation, of praise, of worship.[7]

Wuthnow is on to something. Today it is increasingly common to see runners on the streets, in the park, or on a bike trail wearing headphones, listening to music. Yet not all use of music while running is ritual. Many runners will tell you that they listen to music to make the run more bearable; going for a run is otherwise so boring that listening to music takes their mind off it. Also, many people don't like to run; they are only doing it to burn calories and lose weight, and the music distracts them from the pain of running.

Such uses of music actually present certain hazards. The music masks traffic sounds and often induces daydreaming, which increases the risk of accidents. I have lost count of the number of times I have frightened other runners simply by passing them. They were so involved with their music that they didn't hear me approach, even though I have developed the habit of clearing my throat as a little warning to them that I am coming up quickly behind them. Further, the attitude that the music helps people cope with the boredom or discomfort of running encourages the view that running is just something that must be endured and cannot be fun in its own right. If you begin training gradually, and look for pleasant places to run, you may find that you enjoy running as an activity pursued for its own sake and would rather be aware of your surroundings than distracted by the music. Amby Burfoot, winner of the 1968 Boston Marathon and senior writer for *Runner's World* magazine, has said bluntly, "I do not favor wearing headphones while running—to me, the music gets in the way."[8] And Alberto Salazar, winner of the New York City Marathon and the Boston Marathon, has also expressed concern about listening to music while running, concluding that "personal stereos ... are best restricted to treadmill running."[9]

Although the debate over listening to music while running will most likely continue, when it comes to music and the spirituality of running, two points should be taken into consideration. First, since music and song have always played a significant role in religion and spirituality around the world, there is no reason to suppose it wouldn't be a part of spiritual running as well. And second, even if you feel no desire to take music with you on the road or trail as you run, developing a ritual of listening to music before and after a run can help you prepare for and reflect on your spiritual experiences. The task is to find the right music for you. Many people find the spiritual music from the religious tradition in which they have been raised to be helpful. Others find that music like the theme music from *Chariots of Fire* or *Rocky* helps them get in the right mind-set, while still others find that Melissa Ethridge's "I Run for Life" or "Proud" by Heather Small to be conducive to getting into a spiritual state of mind and creating their own sanctuary out of their run.

MAKING YOUR OWN RITUAL

The key to transforming your run into your own personal sanctuary is to develop your own rituals, and that, in turn, means you need to be intentional about it. There are a number of things you can do for this.

- *Select a special time to run.* Although I recognize that every run has the potential to be a spiritual run, begin by selecting a special time once per week for a run that will include the ritual elements. This may or may not be a time that already has spiritual meaning for you, but it might be best to select a day you are not working or don't have any pressing responsibilities. Also, pick a time of day that is comfortable for you and when you will not encounter a lot of distractions.

- *Select a special place to run.* As I said earlier, pick a route that is pleasant for you to run. It can be hard or easy, as long as it is not something that you will dread. And depending on your fitness level, pick a reasonably long distance. If it is too short, you will spend most of your time warming up. If it is too long, you will grow too tired before it is finished, and this will detract from the experience and also potentially give the run negative associations.

- *Play music.* In the worship services of organized religions like Judaism and Christianity, the service may begin with music and readings from scripture. In a similar way, you can prepare for your run by listening to music, but this is entirely optional. If you decide to play music before your run, you should select music you like. It can be any genre, and perhaps even be a song with a specific message. Take your time and experiment with different kinds of music, and remember that the music should be motivational for your spiritual mind-set. You are using this music to set off regular time from your sacred time and regular space from your sanctuary.

- *Try other activities.* Read scripture, say a prayer, or meditate (more on each of these later in the book).

- *Read your journal.* This may be an appropriate time to read sections of your journal that you find particularly meaningful in a spiritual sense.

- **Run at a good pace—but not too fast.** What you are about to do is neither a race nor a typical training run. You want it to be your spiritual time. So keep your pace deliberate but not hard. You shouldn't run so hard that you could not carry on a conversation with someone else, but not so easy that you hesitate to call it a run and want to call it a jog. Maybe you will find it helpful to read the following lines from *Running and Being* by George Sheehan before you start your run: "I take the universe around me and wrap myself in it and become one with it, moving at a pace which makes me part of it."[10]

> "Regular stretching is critical to injury-free running because limber muscles exert less tension on tendons and ligaments. They're also less prone to muscle pulls, for the simple reason that they're better able to withstand the shock of modest overextension. Stretching also enhances performance. Tight muscles have restricted ranges of motion, constraining your stride length."
> —Alberto Salazar, *Alberto Salazar's Guide to Running: A Champion's Revolutionary Program to Revitalize Your Fitness*

- **Focus your mind.** During your run you can recite poems or sing songs that you have found to be spiritually significant (sing the songs in your imagination if you don't wish to sing them out loud). There may even be phrases that you can repeat to the rhythm of your stride. Concentrate on the words and the message of the poem, song, or phrase that you are taking with you. This practice will help focus your mind as you run.
- **Write in your journal.** Just as you stretch before and after a run, don't forget to write down in your journal the things you experienced on your run. The writings of the saints have become inspirational spiritual reading for many people in traditional religions, and your spiritual journal should become inspirational reading for you.

Your Spiritual Running Journal

Take some time to think about the following questions and write about them in your journal.

- Reflect on the experiences of Henri Nouwen at the Trappist monastery and the young man running in London. Have you ever had an experience like either one of those? Write down the circumstances and describe the event in as much detail as you can remember.
- What are the routines, traditions, and rituals that you have surrounding the practice of running?
- Do you listen to music when you run? Why or why not?
- What kind of music do you like to listen to before or during your runs? How does it make you feel? Is that feeling something that is conducive to spirituality or not?
- How would you describe your personal sanctuary?

On Your Next Run

The next time you go for a run, spend the first half thinking about the things you do over and over in your life. Which are the routines? Which are the traditions? Are there any routines or traditions you would like to omit from your life, or others that you would like to include? Spend the second half of your run focusing on the rituals in your life. Which ones are specifically spiritual or religious in nature? What about them appeals to you most? Why? What can you do to nurture those rituals to keep them fresh so they don't become mere traditions or routines? Are there any rituals from childhood that you miss? If so, is there anything you can do to recapture those rituals? Remember that running itself can also become a

ritual. Which of the suggested methods of making running a ritual works best for you? Try each one on your
subsequent runs and make a practice of doing the one
you like the best.

● ● ● ●

CHAPTER FIVE

PRAYERFUL RUNNING

There are thoughts which are prayers.
There are moments when, whatever the
posture of the body, the soul is on its knees.
—*Victor Hugo*[1]

I am not Catholic, but I attended a Catholic university, which was my first close contact with members of that faith. And even though I considered myself a spiritual person—I attended a church, I believed in God, I read the Bible, and I prayed—I found some of the practices of my Catholic friends interesting.

For example, in the Catholic tradition, the physical gesture of crossing oneself, or making the sign of the cross, precedes a prayer. What I found especially intriguing was seeing numerous runners at track meets cross themselves before a race. I have always been impressed by people whose faith in a higher reality prompts them to make public gestures like that. In some ways I was sorry that as a Baptist I didn't have anything similar.

Since my college days, I have often seen runners cross themselves before going for a run or before a race, and although I myself don't share that practice, I have discovered what many of those runners seem to have always known—praying and running really do seem to go together. Prayer can be a calming activity, and in situations where we can't easily express our feelings of anxiety, thankfulness, awe, and wonder, prayer gives us a means of expression. For those who believe that there is a God, prayer can be a way of letting ourselves know that we are part of something that matters and has meaning.

PRAYER AND SPIRITUALITY

Prayer is an essential part of spirituality. It is perhaps the most important part, because we are not just thinking about God, we are not just seeing or experiencing God in some abstract or detached sense. In prayer we are in conscious communication— or as some would say, *communion*—with God. In a similar vein, a great German philosopher and poet once remarked, "Prayer is to religion, what thinking is to philosophy."[2] There is no true spirituality without prayer.

Prayer is not like a magic spell in which, as long as you say the right words, you get what you want. The idea of prayer is more complicated than that. Someone might even ask, "Why do we have to pray at all? If God is good, all powerful, and all knowing, won't God give us what is best without our having to ask for it?" One response is that God has allowed us quite a bit of freedom as human beings, and we can use this freedom to influence the world around us. In an interesting passage, C. S. Lewis uses the following dialogue to highlight this aspect of prayer:

> "Praying for particular things," said I, "always seems to me like advising God how to run the world. Wouldn't it be wiser to assume that He knows best?"
>
> "On the same principle," said he, "I suppose you never ask a man next to you to pass the salt, because God knows best whether you ought to have salt or not. And I suppose you never take an umbrella, because God knows best whether you ought to be wet or dry."
>
> "That's quite different," I protested.

"I don't see why," said he. "The odd thing is that He should let us influence the course of events at all. But since He lets us do it in one way, I don't see why He shouldn't let us do it in the other."[3]

PRAYER WHILE RUNNING IN THE RAT RACE

As human beings, we don't always feel whole or complete because we often don't see the meaning of what we have to do every day. We go to our jobs and in our spare time try to make a social life, but we don't always see the big picture. Are we really accomplishing anything? To describe this situation, people sometimes speak of being stuck in the rat race.

The phrase *rat race* describes the seemingly endless and pointless activities that we all find ourselves involved with. We feel like rats in a maze, running around in pursuit of a small reward at the end. According to Paul Ulasien, author of *The Corporate Rat Race: The Rats Are Winning*,[4] more than 80 percent of America's workers are dissatisfied with their jobs. In the book he traces the factors that have shaped corporate America today, and he says that "no matter what you do in the rat race, success is not certain, but if you do nothing failure is." Although that is a good point in some respects, it brings to mind the comment by comedienne Lily Tomlin: "The trouble with the rat race is that even if you win, you're still a rat."

Although we might often feel caught in the rat race and can't always see the meaning of what we are doing and how it fits into the bigger picture, many traditions affirm that we can recover the feeling of wholeness through prayer. Prayer helps us establish connections to things and people that were separate. The wholeness that is fostered by prayerful thinking is twofold.

First, prayer brings wholeness to the life of the one who prays. We all wear different hats in our lives (sometimes a great many hats). Each hat stands for a kind of activity in our lives. The trouble for many is that these hats hide who we really are underneath. In the act of prayer, we have an opportunity to take off those hats. We can take time to sort out our lives, to establish a new perspective on who we are, and to think about where we are going. When we think about these things in the presence of God, or informed by our awareness of the Holy, that is prayer. In the act of prayer, all of the separate activities in which we are involved, often without thinking, are brought together. So when we go for a run, we are taking a break from the "rat race," and this break in our normal routine is an ideal opportunity to reflect on who we are.

Second, prayer helps us see the world as a whole. Prayer helps us overcome the ambiguities of life and see the world as sacred and meaningful. The old saying "You can't see the forest for the trees" is an apt description of us: we are so concerned with our little corner of the world that we can easily lose sight of the big picture. Again, when we run, we are given a chance to step out of our normal routine to get a different perspective on ourselves and the world around us. In all of this, the unifying factor is God, and prayer enables us to put our lives and the world around us into perspective.

> "Our motivations for running are absolutely central, because the physical act of running is much easier than the psychological energy it takes to do it.... Take the motivation out of your running, and there is no running."
> —Amby Burfoot, *The Principles of Running: Practical Lessons from My First 100,000 Miles*

PRAYER AS THINKING

Let's get a little more practical. To understand what prayer is, a good starting point is to say that prayer is thinking.[5] And when we run we certainly have time to think. It's fairly obvious that when we pray, we are thinking—that is, there is some sort of brain activity going on. But surely prayer must be of a different kind than the thinking we engage in when, for example, we decide whether we want to run in the morning before going to work or in the evening after we return home from work. Yes, prayer is thinking—but it is a very special sort of thinking.

First, this kind of thinking we call prayer is not just matter-of-fact thinking, but a thinking that involves our emotions and feelings. We feel strongly about things in the world we experience—in short, we feel passionately. When that feeling is sadness or joy about the way things are, we are moving in the direction of prayer.

Second, the kind of thinking we call prayer is also compassionate thinking. To be compassionate is to *feel with* others, thus compassionate thinking is concerned with the situation of others.

Third, prayer is responsible thinking. It is not enough just to feel compassion for the unfortunate situation of others. The spiritual person, along with members of all the major religions, feels a responsibility to do something in the light of that compassion. Thus, prayer and action are closely linked. We don't live our lives in isolation; we live in the real world. And it is difficult to see that world in the right perspective without prayer. Former secretary general of the United Nations Dag Hammarskjöld rightly observed that "in our era the road to holiness necessarily passes through the world of action."[6]

Fourth, prayer is thankful thinking. When we think about the things in the world and in our lives—not only the big things that we have or experience, but the small things that we often overlook—and are thankful for them, once again, this type of thinking approaches prayer.

I have intentionally stated that this type of thinking *approaches* prayer because I believe that many people, even a person who objects to the very notion of prayer, can think passionately, compassionately, responsibly, and thankfully. It is only when this thinking is done in the context of our belief in God or our experience of the sacred reality that it becomes prayer. When we run and see God in the sense I described earlier, and if we think passionately, compassionately, responsibly, and thankfully, *then* we have genuine prayer.

HOW PEOPLE AROUND THE WORLD PRAY

It is staggering how many different ways of praying have developed in the world's religions.[7] Some people pray while standing, others kneel, and still others kneel down and touch their foreheads to the ground. Some cultures insist on keeping their eyes closed during prayer while others pray with eyes open. Some people fold their hands in the act of prayer, others place the palms together when they pray, while others raise their hands skyward. And for each, the method is full of spiritual meaning.

As we think more practically about prayer and *running*, we inevitably ask the question of how to go about doing it. Prayer is one of the things we learn best by doing, not just by reading about it or thinking about it. Perhaps the most important thing to remember about prayer is that you don't need to learn a special method to do it right; you just need to do it! But even granting the truth that we learn to pray by praying, there are some helpful hints and techniques to assist us in prayerful running.

Although we can gain helpful hints from the prayer techniques of some of the world's religions, a lot about how we pray will be determined by what we believe about the universe and about God—as well as the fact that we are running. Thus, it should be fairly obvious that for prayerful running, we have to keep our eyes open, kneeling is not an option, and we should not fold our hands as we pray. But what are some of the things we can learn from the great world religions?

THE RUNNER'S PRAYER FLAG

Prayer flags are popular in certain Buddhist traditions. They are brightly colored rectangular pieces of cloth with woodblock prints of prayers and mantras on them. In Tibet it is believed that as the wind blows, the prayers printed on the flags are carried across the landscape to the gods. The prayer flags are said to promote peace, compassion, wisdom, and strength, bringing health and happiness to those who hang them.

The idea of prayer flags can be adopted for spiritual running. Many runners wear T-shirts with interesting things printed on them. I have seen shirts advertising hospitals, breast cancer research, and scholarship funds—to name only a few. When you see a message like that on another runner's shirt, you can use it as an opportunity to pray for the charity or cause. That can be your prayer flag. I have noticed many people wearing a pin in support of breast cancer research. The spiritual runner can also use that little pink ribbon as a prayer flag and take the opportunity to pray for the families of breast cancer victims, for cancer research hospitals, and for the continued health of cancer survivors.

Boston's Run to Remember, a half-marathon, was organized to honor law enforcement officers from Massachusetts who were killed in the line of duty. Quite often when I am out for a run I see other runners with the handsome long-sleeve T-shirt from that race. On the back of the shirt is the single word *Remember* printed in bold green letters. I use that as a prayer flag to pray for police officers nationwide.

You can also create a runner's prayer flag of your own to wear. Several years ago, my wife was diagnosed with breast cancer. After she underwent a series of surgeries and radiation treatments, I signed up to run in a half-marathon. Before the race I bought a T-shirt and with a black marker printed the words from a Melissa Ethridge song on the front: "I Run for Life." On the back I wrote "For My Wife." My wife had received a clean bill of health from her doctor, so I used this opportunity to pray for the continued health of my wife. As I ran, I received many supportive comments from other runners, which served as further encouragement to me as I prayed for my wife and as I ran the 13.1 miles of the race.

RUNNER'S PRAYER KNOTS AND BEADS

A string of beads has been a material aid for prayer in many cultures. The earliest use of prayer beads can be traced to Hinduism, where they are called *japa mala* (from the Sanskrit words *japa*, meaning "repeating the name of a deity," and *mala,* meaning "garland or wreath"). The most common *japa malas* contain 108 beads, which are made of *rudraksh* seeds, and are used for the repetition of mantras as an aid to meditation. In Islam, prayer beads called *tasbih* or *dhikr* beads are used to recite in Arabic "Glory be to God," "Praise God," and "God is great" thirty-three times each. The one praying uses the beads to keep track of his or her progress through the thirty-three recitations. In the third to fifth centuries, Christian monks tied knots in ropes or cords to assist in the counting of prayers. Later, this custom was adapted to the use of prayer beads, the most celebrated being the rosary in Catholicism. Today, a variety of other Christian denominations use prayer beads and prayer ropes as aids in the recitation of prayers.

Although it may not be too convenient to carry prayer beads with you when you run, there are alternatives. I have a friend who makes a prayer list for each week. On days that she goes for a spiritual run, she takes a small piece of cord and ties a number of knots in it, each knot corresponding to one of things she has to pray for. The cord is light, so it is no trouble to carry with her. As she runs, she holds one knot at a time and uses it as a reminder of what to pray for. The next time she goes for a run, she either reties the cord, adding or leaving off knots, or uses a fresh piece of cord.

PACE BAND, PRAYER BAND

If you have run a marathon or half-marathon, you know that a pace band is a slip of water-resistant paper you wear on your wrist during the race. It is printed with certain times correlated to each mile of the race to help you keep the pace to finish in your desired time. So if you wish to finish a marathon in four hours, your pace band will indicate that you should complete your first mile in 9:09 minutes, your second mile in 18:18 minutes, your third mile in 27:27 minutes, and so on. As you pass each mileage post, you can compare your actual time with the time printed on your pace band and adjust your pace accordingly.

Recently, some marathon runners have adapted this idea and have made their pace band into a prayer band. Along with their pace time, they list people or things they want to pray for at each mile of the marathon. It is a constructive use of their time, and it also helps the time pass more quickly. This method was described by Kristin Armstrong, contributing editor for *Runner's World* magazine:

> I heard of a runner who made a marathon prayer list of 26 people and dedicated a mile to each person. The only thing I didn't like about this idea was that I hadn't thought of it myself. Paige and I consolidated our prayer lists and beside each mile marker on her pace band was a split time and names of family members or friends. We dedicated an early mile to a couple struggling with their marriage; one for our coach Cassie; one for our brothers. As our prayers and miles intensified, our talking subsided. The silence between us grew as we pressed on with miles for our parents, for Paige's husband, Jamil, for my children's father, Lance, and for Eric, the new man in my life who was waiting for me at the finish line.... When we travel to races together, I'm in charge of hotel and dinner reservations and Paige is the boss of race day. We get along just fine this way. Paige wears the pace band, keeps the splits, shouts whether I get Gatorade or water, and tells me when to eat a Fig Newton or take a Gu. This time she also announced the names of the people we were running each mile for.[8]

A RUNNER'S PRAYER

When you go for a prayerful run, you can pray as if you are talking to someone right next to you. The words aren't important, but you don't have to make up your own prayer extemporaneously. You can pray a prayer you have heard before, or one that you learned in your spiritual tradition. I know people who recite the Lord's Prayer on their run and others who have memorized prayers from spiritual leaders in their tradition.

Last time I checked, there is no patron saint for runners. In the Catholic Church the closest one is St. Sebastian, the patron saint of athletes. We fare quite a bit better if we are looking for a runner's prayer. The one I found most interesting was published in *Day by Day: The Notre Dame Prayerbook for Students*:

> Run by my side—live in my heartbeat; give strength to my steps.
>
> As the cold confronts me, as the wind pushes me, I know you surround me.
>
> As the sun warms me, as the rain cleanses me, I know you are touching me, challenging me, loving me.
>
> And so I give you this run; thank you for matching my stride. Amen[9]

Your Spiritual Running Journal

Before moving on to the next chapter, take some time to think about the following questions and write about them in your journal.

- Do you ever pray? What are the circumstances that normally lead you to pray (such as in time of need, when you feel thankful, when you just feel good, or something else)?
- In light of this discussion of prayer, what do you think is going on when you pray?

- What effects do you see when you pray? Do you see your prayers answered in external events? In a change in internal attitude and perspective? Both?

On Your Next Run

The next time you go for a run, spend the first third of your run considering the role of prayer in your life. Do you like formalized prayers that you can repeat, or do you prefer praying spontaneously according to circumstances? What obstacles do you encounter when you pray? What distractions? What conditions do you find conducive to prayer? Spend the second third of your run carefully observing the world around you as you run and think about the following questions. What can you use as your own "prayer flag"? Consider the kinds of things or the people you would pray for if you were going to use a set of prayer beads or knots or a prayer band. Why not try one of those on your next run? Spend the final third of your run actually praying. Bring your thoughts into focus with the awareness that you are doing so in the presence of God. What kinds of things will you pray for? Notice how your thoughts are interacting with the environment as you run. What is your experience like?

● ● ● ●

MEDITATIVE RUNNING

Those who eat too much or eat too little, who sleep too much or sleep too little, will not succeed in meditation. But those who are temperate in eating and sleeping, work and recreation, will come to the end of sorrow through meditation.

—*Bhagavad Gita*[1]

One hour's meditation on the work of the Creator is better than seventy years of prayer.

—*Muhammad*[2]

Prayer is vital to spirituality, but as we pray, we discover that our experience deepens into a more meditative state of mind than mere thinking. This deeper state is uniquely potent; in fact, in the words of the Prophet Muhammad, seven decades of prayer is equal to a single hour of meditation.

In this chapter I would like to introduce the idea of *meditative running*. Since meditation is a slippery sort of word—it can mean different things to different people—I would like to make as clear as possible what I mean by it.

The word *meditation* most commonly means "to muse," "to ponder," "to reflect," or "to consider." Although some traditions teach a meditation of emptying the mind, I am promoting a meditation where the mind is full, but focused. But the meditation I advocate here is not just an intellectual activity. Rather, meditation starts with the mind, but also necessarily involves the heart. It is a journey within yourself, with the ultimate goal of *enlightenment*—the solution of spiritual or ethical problems, a new perception allowing you to see reality in a new light, and the realization that all things work together as part of a whole. For those who are religious, this also means finding God's guidance or God's message for us. But don't let this description discourage you; meditative running can be practiced with equal value by anyone.

ANONYMOUS MEDITATION

Looking back at my early years of serious running in high school and college, I have come to realize that even then I was doing a form of running meditation without knowing it. Every time I was troubled by parents, schoolwork, a girlfriend, or something else and went out for a run, I was doing a form of meditation—what I call anonymous meditation. Even though I wasn't intentionally meditating, going for a run focused my mind on a particular problem, and I would often come back refreshed, feeling better about myself and the situation.

> "Letting my mind free-float during a walk or run is therapeutic for me, it's another form of dreaming. The demons come out, the creativity comes in."
> —Kathrine Switzer, *Running and Walking for Women Over 40*

Recently, I have discovered that anonymous meditation is widespread among most runners. As part of the course I teach, "The Spirituality of Running," students are asked to write an essay about a spiritual experience they have had while running. Time and time again, they describe situations where they had a problem and went for a run. During the course of the run, they had the opportunity to think their problem through, and somehow when they finished their run, they felt better about their situation. The details may be different, but the spiritual benefits of anonymous meditative running are common. Once we can recognize what meditation is and how best to practice it, we can discover new depths in the art of spiritual running, whether or not we are religious.

THE NEED TO LOOK INSIDE

So often in our society we are encouraged to avoid doing certain chores and to allow someone else to do them for us. If we are too busy to prepare meals, we can order take-out food. Even cooking at home has been simplified. If you want a home-baked cake, all you have to do is open a package that someone else has made, add one or two ingredients, and—*voilà*—you have a "homemade" cake. But this is not the same as making the effort to pick up a cookbook, find a recipe, and make a cake from scratch. We may gain convenience, but we lose some of the spirit.

This trend for convenience has extended to the realm of religion and spirituality as well. Too often we sit back and allow someone else to do all the "work" for us. Some contemporary worship services with massive multimedia capabilities resemble concerts more than a worship service, which may tend to fuel the idea that religion should be fun and (just like a concert) anonymous. We don't even have to *go* to a place of worship, all we have to do is turn on the television, and we can tune in to programming that suits our spiritual tastes of the moment. Some people seem to feel that their spiritual leader is supposed to solve all their problems for them.

I think that when we don't engage the in hard work of spirituality ourselves, we miss out on some wonderful opportunities. If we are coping with a problem and leave the solutions up to somebody else, we may treat the symptoms of the problem, but we will miss the root of the problem and it will persist. That is where meditation comes into play. There is a very nice story in the book *Zen Flesh, Zen Bones* that tells of a man named Daiju who traveled a great distance to learn from the Zen master Baso.

> Baso asked, "What do you seek?"
> "Enlightenment," replied Daiju.
> "You have your own treasure house. Why do you search outside?" Baso asked.
> Daiju inquired: "Where is my treasure house?"
> Baso answered: "What you are asking *is* your treasure house."
> Daiju was enlightened! Ever after he urged his friends: "Open your own treasure house and use those treasures."[3]

What this story tells us is that the true spiritual guide is the one who offers us a chance to stay alone and take the risk of entering into our own experience instead of advising us what to do or to whom to go. The spiritual writer Henri Nouwen tells us that the true spiritual guide is one who helps us realize that "pouring little bits of water on our dry land does not help, but that we will find a living well if we reach deep enough under the surface of our complaints."[4]

Meditation is the way we reach inside ourselves to find spiritual enlightenment in times of need. But this is no easy or quick fix: the process of meditation may not be difficult, but it is not always convenient or fun. Yet by making the effort, we discover meaning in light of our current situation and experiences. I believe that as runners we are in an ideal position to do just that.

Although many books have been written on the subject, how to meditate falls into two basic categories. First, there is the meditation that uses a sound, word, phrase, or sentence to focus our thoughts. These sounds or words are called mantras, and they usually have some religious meaning. By repeating a mantra, you can develop great powers of concentration. The second kind of meditation uses a reading or story to focus thought. The reading can be from scripture or some other literature. In either case, although the actual meditation is quite simple, it takes practice and discipline. And if you have the discipline to run regularly, you certainly have the discipline to meditate.

The aim of meditation is to bring enlightenment and harmony to us as human creatures—a harmony of body, mind, and spirit. In this way, meditation can be beneficial to everyone regardless of your specific spiritual path. But for all forms of *religious* meditation, the aim is to allow God's presence in and with us to become the reality that gives meaning to everything that we do. This was expressed classically by the psalmist who wrote, "Be still and know that I am God" (Ps. 46:10). Thus, religious or non-religious meditation is about learning to listen—to listen to our deepest self and to be attentive to the sacred reality.

SEED MANTRAS

The most basic type of mantra is called a seed mantra. These are the basic sounds we make intentionally that somehow make us feel better. When you stretch in the morning, do you make a nice satisfying groan? That is like a seed mantra—however, you probably don't repeat it. There are also seed mantras you can use when you run: sounds you can make over and over in a meditative way to help you feel better. They express the good feeling that you have when you run, and by repeating it, you contribute to the experience.

When I am alone running in the woods, and I feel like everything is good, I take a very deep breath and let it out slowly with a low sigh. It is for me an expression of the joy of running and of the freedom that running represents; it is also an expression of the joy of my body and especially of my legs and lungs; an expression of the joy of existence. Making this sound contributes to the overall experience.

The next time you go for a run and you feel good, express yourself! What sound do you make? It is important for you to find your own sound. Finding this sound can be a joy in itself, but for those of us who are religious, it can also contribute to our feeling in the presence of God.

CONVENTIONAL MANTRAS

A second type of mantra uses a special word or phrase to concentrate your thought. Probably the most famous mantra of Buddhism is *om mani padme hum*. This is particularly popular among Tibetan Buddhists and is said to bring peace to the one who repeats it with regularity. Interestingly, among Hindus and Buddhists, the saying of mantras is often linked to the physical stretches and poses collectively known as yoga. So we shouldn't be surprised that linking this type of mantra with running is also very helpful.

Even though some religious traditions believe that the saying of a mantra is effective and helpful in itself independent of the person saying it, there seems to be a greater consensus among those who practice meditation that you should use mantras that are meaningful to you. So for most of us, the repetition of the phrase *om mani padme hum* will not get us very far in the practice of meditation. Similarly, if you are Roman Catholic, saying the Hail Mary in Latin—if you never learned Latin—would have little or no meaning for you. In either case, for most people, the repetition of a phrase or sentence is not very helpful to true personal meditation unless you understand what it means and that meaning resonates deeply within you.

Within Judaism, the repetition of the Shema, a passage from the Torah that reads, "Hear, O Israel! The Lord is our God, the Lord is one" (Deut. 6:4), declaring the oneness of the Holy One of Israel, can be used as a mantra. It is interesting that although the Shema is often looked upon as a prayer, it is not addressed to God, but is an admonition to all Jews to remember who God is. In the Muslim tradition, particularly among Sufis, chants of the ninety-nine names of Allah are a kind of mantra. And among Christians, there are many well-known mantras such as the Jesus Prayer and the Hail Mary. Particularly interesting forms of meditation using mantras were taught by Thomas Merton, a Trappist monk, and Dom John Main, a Benedictine priest.[5] Eleven years before his death in 1968, Thomas Merton had come to use the Jesus Prayer of Orthodox Christianity as his mantra, and John Main taught the use of the Aramaic phrase *maranatha*, which means "O Lord come." If any of these phrases resonates with meaning for you, repeating it respectfully while running can become your mantra. Or you can come up with your own mantra.

CUSTOMIZE YOUR PERSONAL MANTRA

Pause for a few minutes now to think about what a mantra is, and try to find one that suits you. Remember that a mantra is supposed to focus your thoughts on a particular thing—a concern, a personal problem, a question, or the meaning of your life. It can be religious or not, and it can be very simple. In fact, simplicity of thought and expression is desirable. Here I list a number of simple mantras to give you some ideas.

Nonreligious Mantras

- Running brings peace, running brings calm.
- Peace to all.
- I open to what is.
- May all be well.

Religious Mantras

- God is with me.
- God will help.
- Knowing others is wisdom, knowing the Self is enlightenment.

Scriptural Mantras from Different Traditions

- This is the day the Lord has made; let us rejoice and be glad in it. (Ps. 118:24)
- God is our refuge and strength. (Ps. 46:1)

- Be still and know that I am God. (Ps. 46:10)
- Come near to God and God will come near to you. (James 4:8)
- God is light. (1 John 1:5)
- He is the First and the Last. (Qur'an 57:3)
- It is good to tame the mind. (Dhammapada 3:1)

It is helpful to select a word or phrase that is easy to remember and easy to repeat during the run. As you run, you can say it out loud or silently to yourself, but say it slowly and deliberately—preferably to the rhythm of your running. Just like a pair of running shoes, it may take a few days to break the mantra in and for you to feel comfortable with it. You may find that the mantra you chose is just not right for you. If that's the case, don't be discouraged; simply choose a new one.

Repeat the mantra as you run, out loud or silently to yourself, and think about the word or words. You have come to your sanctuary—running—and are using the mantra as a tool to focus your thoughts. When you sit at home or in your office, there are many distractions that can easily prevent you from the type of concentration that is necessary. Likewise, the effort of thinking about the words or the sound of a mantra, if it has meaning for you, blocks out other thoughts and helps you focus your mind. Although this kind of meditation takes practice, even the first time you do it may show results of feeling more refreshed mentally afterward.

DIVINE READING, DIVINE RUNNING

The second basic type of meditation is *lectio divina*, which means "divine reading." This method was developed in the Middle Ages when monks read from the Bible and then spent time concentrating on that reading, looking deeply into themselves in the light of what they read. It was for them a prelude to prayer, as it can be for us as well.

Important for all *lectio divina* is *not* to master the meaning of the words per se, but to allow the words you read to speak to you and challenge you. This is what I call reading something spiritually. If you received a love letter from someone you care about, it wouldn't matter how an English teacher might analyze it. If you care about that person, the analysis by the English teacher is irrelevant to you. The letter speaks to you on an entirely different level. In short, then, "spiritual reading is a reading in which we allow the word to read and interpret us."[6]

As a spiritual runner, you can practice a kind of *lectio divina* as well. Just select something to read before going out for a run. The reading can be from scripture, from a religious book, or even something you found in a newspaper. What makes this true meditation is that you take time to yourself and go to your sanctuary, the run, to ponder and reflect on the meaning of a specific reading to your life.

WHAT SHOULD YOU READ?

The most important aspect of finding something to read for a *lectio divina* is not necessarily what you read, but your ability to read it spiritually. That said, perhaps the most obvious selection for a *lectio divina* is a passage of scripture—which scripture you choose, of course, may depend on the religious tradition you were raised in or are most familiar with. A wealth of devotional literature written within different religious traditions is also available. This literature includes short passages, often reflections on scripture, written by people trained (or at least well read) in a particular tradition. These readings are easily digested and lend themselves well to running meditation.

Further sources of material to read in preparation for a meditative run are works of theology written by great teachers either past or present and even works of philosophy. The important thing is to find a passage that resonates with you. With that in mind, there is nothing to prevent you from selecting a poem, a short story, or even the words of a song as the basis of your meditative run.

A final source of reading material for a meditative run is newspaper or news magazine articles. There is so much going on in the world that is of spiritual importance—events related to ethics and morality—that the reading of specific news items can be an extremely fruitful source for meditative running.

Lectio divina as running meditation is not done in isolation from the things of the world. Henri Nouwen tells the story of a priest who cancelled his subscription to the *New York Times*. The priest did this because he thought that "the endless stories about war, crime, power games, and political manipulation only disturbed his mind and heart and prevented him from meditation and prayer."[7] It is so unfortunate that he felt that way! The real spiritual life does not exclude the outside world. It makes us alert and aware of what's happening in the world and helps us think responsibly. Only by being aware of the world and what is happening in it can we meditate on how we fit into that world. Only by meditating on problems can we try to find the solutions. Only by meditating on scripture can we truly appropriate its message and see what it means for us. At a time when people are becoming increasingly dissatisfied with organized religion, running meditation can be a rewarding spiritual discipline.

RUNNING MEDITATION

The actual practice of running meditation has at least three parts. These parts are like the movements of a symphony—each is separate, but each, in its own way, contributes to the whole. And in the end we look at the whole and what it does for us.

The first part is the preparation for the run itself. If you are doing a *lectio divina*, select the passage you wish to read and read it thoughtfully. Prepare for your run with a time of stretching, perhaps listening to music that you enjoy that is also conducive to a spiritual attitude. Before you start a meditative run, it is usually helpful to say a short prayer that briefly states your spiritual goal for this particular run. And if you will be using a mantra, think of what mantra you will use before you actually head out.

The second part of the meditative run is the run itself. As you begin running, remember that a meditative run takes time. Keep in mind that you don't have to run at a very fast pace. You should be running fast enough to enjoy the speed, but not so fast that you couldn't talk comfortably if you wanted to. Also, it needs to be a reasonably long run for you, so it probably will be more than a run around the block. But this is very individual and will vary depending on how fast you run and what shape you are in.

George Sheehan had great insight into spiritual aspects of running. In his book *Running and Being*, he stated an extremely important principle of spiritual running generally, but meditative running in particular. "The first half hour of my run," he wrote, "is for my body. The last half hour, for my soul. In the beginning the road is a miracle of solitude and escape. In the end it is a miracle of discovery and joy."[8] In his own way, he was telling us that the run itself has two halves. During the first half, we are just getting warmed up, both physically and mentally. It is during the second half of our run that we can expect the most spiritual benefit.

> "The weekly long run should be part of every runner's training program, even if you're not building up to a marathon. Long runs improve aerobic capacity and fat-burning ability and increase weight loss and musculo-skeletal strength. And you don't need to cover 20 miles at a time. Basically, a long run is any workout that's 50 percent longer than your average run."
> —Amby Burfoot, *The Principles of Running: Practical Lessons from My First 100,000 Miles*

Finally, the third part of the meditative run is when you have completed your run and take time to stretch. Stretching before and after a long-distance run is always important. For the spiritual runner, it is good to recognize these as part of the entire experience. If you like, you can listen to the same music you were listening to before you began your run. But most important, reflect on your run. Was it spiritually productive? This isn't always easy to answer and can be very subjective. How do you feel now that it is finished? Take time to write down your thoughts in your spiritual journal. Reading your journal later on can be a spiritual experience as well.

Don't be discouraged if you don't have wonderful, extraordinary experiences every time you meditate. Expect some of your meditative runs to be dull and uneventful. In this regard, the great Lutheran pastor Dietrich Bonhoeffer, has some good advice:

> It is not necessary that we should have any unexpected, extraordinary experiences in meditation. This can happen, but if it does not, it is not a sign that the meditation period has been useless.... There will be times when we feel a great spiritual dryness ... even an inability to meditate.... Above all, we must not allow them to keep us from adhering to our meditation period with great patience and fidelity.[9]

If we don't have any extraordinary experiences when we go for a meditative run, at worst we will get a good run in, and what's wrong with that? But at best, we will have discovered a side of our running and of ourselves that we never knew existed; a side that we can turn to for the rest of our lives.

Your Spiritual Running Journal

Before going on to the next chapter, reflect on the following questions and write about them in your journal.

- Have you ever meditated before in the sense that I am talking about in this chapter? Have you ever had what I call an anonymous meditative experience? Describe it in detail. How did it make you feel?

- The next time you are troubled by something you read in the newspaper, think about what it is that is troubling you and write your thoughts in your journal. Is this a spiritual problem? If you think it is, try to understand why it is a spiritual problem. Then, before you go for a run, read this entry in your journal and meditate on the spiritual issues. Don't be too analytical; just think about the problem and try to open yourself up to the answer.

- If you make a habit of reading from religious literature (some scripture, or perhaps devotional literature), go for a run right after reading and meditate on what you read. When you return from the run, write down any thoughts on what you experienced.

On Your Next Run

The next time you go for a run, begin by selecting a text and read it using the method of *lectio divina*. Or select a mantra that you want to repeat on your run. As you begin the run, start out with a brief prayer as you practiced in the previous chapter. This time, focus less on observing the process and, instead, let yourself go into it. If you are saying your mantra, let the rhythm of your feet and breathing envelope you and establish a smooth pattern to your mantra. If you have done a *lectio divina*, ponder the spiritual meaning of the passage you read. In either case, allow the problems and concerns of your day or week to flow out with your breath and moving feet. Let the wisdom that is already resident in your "treasure house" emerge. Don't resist what comes up. Allow the experience to deepen into meditation.

When you finish your run, you may wish to spend some more time in prayer, but also be sure to return to your spiritual running journal and record what your experience was like. On your subsequent run, consider whether the mantra you chose was as effective as you thought it would be. If it was, go running and use it again. If not, try a new one, or try a different text to use for your *lectio divina* reading. Give each selection a chance to work, but don't be afraid to experiment until you find the right combination that works for you.

● ● ● ●

SACRAMENTAL RUNNING

Earth's crammed with heaven,
And every common bush afire with God;
But only he who sees, takes off his shoes,
The rest sit round it and pluck blackberries ...
—Elizabeth Barrett Browning[1]

Late in the summer of 2005, one of the strongest Atlantic hurricanes ever recorded made landfall on the Gulf coast of Louisiana and Mississippi. Meteorolgists named the hurricane Katrina, and it became the costliest and one of the deadliest in the history of the United States. New Orleans was particularly hardhit. There was flooding throughout the city and not only did many people lose their homes, but more than a thousand people lost their lives. All of us were horror struck as we read and watched the news of this disaster and its aftermath. Several weeks later, I was watching the *Today Show* on television when they interviewed a number of people who had survived the hurricane and were in New York to run in the New York City Marathon that was going to take place on November 6.

A few of these runners explained that they were members of a running club in New Orleans and had been preparing for more than a year to run in the New York race. After the hurricane hit, however, they decided to drop their plans. How could they concentrate on their training and justify all the time they were spending preparing for the marathon, they asked themselves, when they were surrounded by all the destruction and devastation in New Orleans? But giving it some more thought, they decided to follow through with their plans and run the marathon anyway. After all, one person said, the long runs during training became for them a welcome escape from reality.

An escape from reality! I was taken aback by that phrase. My first thought was that those long runs do not need to be seen as an escape *from* reality. In the midst of the devastation, pain, and sorrow caused by the hurricane, those long runs could be seen as an escape *to* reality—an opportunity to look beyond the destruction and see the sacred reality all about them.

In an earlier chapter, I discussed the idea of "seeing" God while out on a run. Here I want to talk about another kind of experience, a more intimate experience of God that we can have while running—what I call sacramental running.

There are many different ways we can know something. We can memorize facts. We can accumulate a wealth of theoretical knowledge. We can even "see" God in the world around us and be convinced that the Divine infuses everything.

But these ways of knowing are from the head and are different than the kind of knowing a sacramental run can bring about—an experiential kind of knowing that involves your head but also involves your heart, your emotions, even your instincts and intuition. It's a fuller kind of knowing. It's like the difference between learning about a person by reading his or her résumé and knowing that person on every level because you are married to him or her. In that second way, the experience of the other person is so direct and intimate that often words aren't necessary— sometime words aren't even possible. We feel all our feelings more intensely—wonder, ecstasy, sorrow, disappointment, hope— everything that makes us human. This is the kind of experience of the Sacred that a sacramental run can give us.

WONDER AND AWE

In order to understand what this sacramental experience means to us as runners, we should explore a little of how we experience the world around us and how we experience ourselves as human beings. The more that scientists study the universe, the more we recognize that it is far more complex than we will ever know. One of the great minds in the world of science, Isaac Newton, recognizing this unimaginable complexity, once remarked:

> I do not know what I may appear to the world; but to myself I seem to have been only like a boy playing on the seashore, and diverting myself in now and then finding a smoother pebble or a prettier shell than ordinary, whilst the great ocean of truth lay all undiscovered before me.[2]

Human beings are looking for that which transcends us. We are restless in our search for God, even if we don't always understand the source of our restlessness. St. Augustine recognized this more than 1,500 years ago when he wrote, "Lord ... you have made us for yourself, and our hearts are restless until they find their rest in you."[3]

There are times when we can really see and feel God's presence in our surroundings. Such moments are called revelation. When God is revealed *and* when we are ready and waiting, the sign is received. Experiences like that are called sacramental. They are possible not only because the Divine reaches out to us, but also because we have been given the capacity—the grace, if you will—to respond.

For some, when they have such a direct and intense encounter with the Holy, this kind of sacramental experience (whether achieved through running or some other activity) is a kind of conversion experience. The Holy is no longer just an object of study, something about which they learn information. The sacred reality has become something, or rather someone, that actually moves in their lives and changes them. When this happens, people often say that God "spoke" to them, or that God "touched their hearts." What they are trying to describe is an *experience of God*. But for many people who have such an experience—perhaps most people—this remains a one-time experience that they don't consciously attempt to repeat or develop.

DOORS AND WINDOWS TO THE SACRED

But others yearn to have such experiences again, and they sometimes do some pretty interesting things to try to repeat or enhance that experience. In Hinduism and Buddhism, forms of yoga and meditation are believed to be a path to such experiences. Judaism, Christianity, and Islam each have their own spiritual disciplines that encourage these encounters. These practices often use physical objects to mediate the reality of God to human beings. Such practices are called *sacraments* or *sacramental practices*.

The word *sacrament* (*sacramentum*) was coined in Christian theology, and originally it simply meant "a sacred or holy thing." By the fifth century, St. Augustine defined a sacrament as a "visible sign of an invisible reality,"[4] and this is the basic meaning it still has today. Under this definition, just about anything in the world can become a sacrament, since everything in the world was created by God and can, in that sense, be considered sacred or holy—even a "sign" for God. This is what the German-American theologian Paul Tillich was referring to when he wrote: "In every religion the experience of the holy is mediated by some piece of finite reality. Everything can become a medium of revelation, a bearer of divine power.... Through stars and stones, trees and animals ... the holy can encounter us."[5]

More specifically, the Christian tradition includes a number of sacraments, such as baptism and the Lord's Supper. Christians generally believe that a sacrament is a ritual in which we experience a direct contact with God through physical objects. In baptism, for example, the water mediates divine grace, and in the Lord's Supper, the bread and wine represent the very body and blood of Jesus. Oxford professor John Macquarrie wrote that it is the purpose of all sacraments "to make the things of this world so transparent that in them and through them we know God's presence and activity in our very midst."[6] But although the word *sacrament* was created as a term within Christianity, sacraments can be found in all religions. The point is that all of the things in the world, being created by God, can function as "doors to the sacred," as one writer has expressed it,[7] or can become "transparent," like windows, to the reality of the God who made them.

But for a growing number of people in our society, participating in the rituals of traditional organized religions has lost its power to connect us to the Sacred and participation in them is meaningless. It is as if windows that were once clean and clear have become so dirty that you can't see through them any more. Or as if the doors through which God could touch us are now closed and locked.

What we need is some way to clean the windows so that they can be the means of seeing the reality of the beautiful world outside, or to unlock the doors so that the Sacred can once again come to us. In a variety of cultures, and at different times, this realization has led men and women to run as a means of experiencing the world in that sacramental way. By using our bodies in this way, we place ourselves in a position to experience many of the things of this world—the road under our feet, the trees we pass by on our favorite trail, the sun as it is rising or setting, animals such as dogs, cats, squirrels, and chipmunks, and even people. Before, you may have sensed the Divine present in each of these things, but on a sacramental run, the divine presence reaches right through these doors and windows and seizes you.

In this way, running can become a sacramental practice. The question is, then, since we *can* experience God through everything, when we are out on a run is there anything we can do to enhance our chances of having such a sacramental experience? I think there is.

THE RUNNER'S HIGH

The first thing is not to *try* to have such an experience. Whenever I talk with runners about spirituality and running, the conversation almost invariably turns to the so-called runner's high. What is the runner's high? In *The Runner's Guide to the Meaning of Life*, Amby Burfoot, 1968 Boston Marathon winner and senior editor for *Runner's World* magazine, wrote that "a runner's high is a special experience that most runners don't have all the time (an important point) but do get at irregular, unpredictable intervals."[8] He continued by saying that "the true runner's high is a zone that we enter when everything seems to click perfectly, when time stands still, and when we can run almost without effort."[9] An interesting thing about this is that Burfoot also admits that it happens for him *at most* about one or two times a year.

Although this is not exactly the same thing as the intimate experience of a sacramental run, there are some similarities. First, just as nobody knows exactly what causes the runner's high,[10] nobody can give you a precise formula for how the intimate experience of God can be achieved. And second, as with the runner's high, you can't count on having this kind of experience every time you go out for a run. A sacramental run can be a significant part of the spirituality of running and one we should prepare for, but it is not an experience that anyone can guarantee. That is because it involves a reality outside ourselves. Whereas we can usually "see" the Holy in our surroundings if we make a conscious effort (as discussed in chapter 3), experiencing the Divine in a sacramental way is not something we can make happen. We can prepare for it, we can go for our runs regularly and intentionally, but in the end, it is not something that we can induce.

FINDING A BALANCE

The second thing we can do is allow our runs to help us maintain a balance between the different areas of our lives.

It is interesting that the universe seems to present itself to us in two ways—or at least we divide our experience of the world into two categories, which go by a variety of paired names: the secular and the sacred, the natural and the supernatural, or the material world and the spiritual world. But remember, it is only one world—we just experience it in two ways. We often emphasize the material aspects of it at the expense of the spiritual, or vice versa.

In our current culture, people seem to have given priority to the physical. People value the advances of the natural sciences and success in business, and are more concerned with physical appearance and the accumulation of material possessions. Spiritual concerns have been marginalized and, for many people, are close to being pushed out entirely.

"Many women take up running to lose weight—with good reason, since running is one of the most efficient and best calorie-burning activities around. What often happens, though, is that once a woman begins running, she discovers many rewards she didn't expect. Running relieves her stress. It gives her more energy, makes her feel good physically. Weight loss becomes secondary. She continues to run and to improve, and she loses a few pounds, even though that's no longer the focus. She feels good about her body and about herself."

—Claire Kowalchik, *The Complete Book of Running for Women*

But in some places and times, the spiritual side has been emphasized at the expense of the physical. In India, for example, there are people called *sadhus* who believe that salvation or enlightenment can only be found by denying the world. Such people fast and deny bodily desires, while embracing poverty and even homelessness. In Christianity, some men and women separate themselves from society by entering monasteries and convents and taking vows of poverty and chastity.

At their extremes, both approaches are unhelpful, for each in its way denies a valid part of who we are as human beings. We have to accept that as long as we are alive, we shall constantly experience the tensions between spiritual and material, soul and body. It is our nature, as human beings, to live in these tensions, and we must seek a right balance between the two. At the end of his commencement address delivered at Harvard University, Nobel Prize–winner Alexander Solzhenitsyn made the following comment:

> [The world] has reached a major watershed in history, equal in importance to the turn from the Middle Ages to the Renaissance. It will demand from us a spiritual effort; we shall have to rise to a new height of vision, to a new level of life, where our physical nature will not be cursed, as in the Middle Ages, but even more importantly, our spiritual being will not be trampled upon, as in the Modern Era.[11]

In religion, the sacraments are ways of honoring and balancing both the material and the spiritual in a single act.

Running can do this, too. It is this duality of existence that is, in some sense, why we run in the first place. Running is a natural human activity; it is a physical activity that we have in common with other animals. But running is not just a physical activity; it is a spiritual activity as well. I feel good when I do it *right*; I have a feeling of, shall I say, *ecstasy* in the middle of a long run through the forest when I am in good shape. And I am dumbfounded by people who run a lot and yet describe running as a painful experience and say they have to "run through" the pain. That may be true and necessary for the competitive runner, but for those of us who just love to run, we celebrate the whole of our existence—body and soul.

As human beings, we not only experience this duality in the world around us, but in ourselves as well. For thousands of years, people have talked about human beings as a combination of *body* and *soul*, that is, composed of two distinct entities. More recently, though, psychologists have sought to express this distinction in a way that highlights our essential unity by speaking of us as *psychosomatic* beings. That is, these two aspects of our being, the body (*soma*) and soul (*psyche*), the spiritual and the physical, coexist and are united in us. I think it is important to note that each side of this duality also has an affect on the other. Doctors speak of psychosomatic diseases in which the mind is able to make the body sick, and sometimes the reverse is true, and a physical condition can affect us in a psychological way (which explains why medications—which affect the body—are sometimes used to treat unfavorable conditions of the mind, such as depression).

NOT SO DIFFERENT AFTER ALL

Just as the two halves of our selves are deeply connected, so too are the dualistic halves of the world closely linked. In fact, through sacraments, the material world can become a way *to* God. It can become a door or channel of communication. In this way, our spiritual well-being demands that we recognize and cherish the visible things of the world as things that are made by God and that provide access to God.

I want to stress, however, that in these cases God, or the Sacred, has the initiative. A sacrament is not a magical way of conjuring up the Holy for our purposes. We cannot open or shut the doors. God comes to us through them, and part of the wondrous mystery of it all is that this reality can also come to us through unexpected doors. After all, God has many names.[12]

BEEN PLUCKING BLACKBERRIES TOO LONG

If we want to have such a sacramental experience, we need to be alert. Well over three thousand years ago, a man named Moses was working as a shepherd in the Middle East, in a remote area near Mount Horeb on the Sinai Peninsula. It was there that he encountered God in a highly unusual way: he met God in a bush. In itself, coming upon a bush was not unusual, even a bush on fire. Brush fires would not have been unusual out in the desert where Moses was. What made this event unusual was that the bush wasn't being consumed by the flames—it wasn't burning up. As Moses approached this curiosity, he heard a voice from the bush call him by name. The voice instructed him to take off his shoes because the ground he was walking on was holy. What made the ground holy, according to the story found in the Bible in the Book of Exodus (3:1–22), was the presence of God, speaking to Moses from the bush.

Some three thousand years after Moses's encounter with God, the famous nineteenth-century English poet Elizabeth Barrett Browning wrote the epigraph that appears at the head of this chapter. She seems to be telling us that we have the potential to experience the Sacred in *everything*. But that potential is not always realized. There are lots of people who don't *see* God, don't *feel* God, and don't *encounter* God at all. For Browning, these people just sit around and "pluck blackberries." Well, many people are coming to realize that we've been plucking blackberries for too long.[13]

Your Spiritual Running Journal

Before moving on to the next chapter, think about the following questions and write your reflections in your journal.

- Have you ever had a sacramental experience (while on a run or not)? If you never have, can you imagine what it must be like? Try to describe that experience.
- In the light of this chapter, what do you think you would have to do to prepare yourself for a sacramental run?

- Are there any places or times that would be more conducive to a sacramental experience for you? Why do you think this is?

On Your Next Run

The next time you go for a run, prepare yourself for a possible sacramental experience. Spend the first third of your run pondering the balance, or lack thereof, between the spiritual and material in your life. Spend the next third of your run concentrating on "seeing" God in your surroundings as you practiced in chapter 3. Where do you find your eyes drawn repeatedly? The clouds? The trees? What draws your eyes there? Spend the final third of your run simply opening up to whatever you see, experience, or feel as you run. Don't *try* to feel anything, just feel. Be open to the possibility that every bush you pass (and everything else, for that matter) is afire with God. What is your experience like?

● ● ● ●

CHAPTER EIGHT

RUNNING AS PILGRIMAGE

The word religion *points to that area of human
experience where one way or another we come upon
Mystery as a summons to pilgrimage.*

—*Frederick Buechner*[1]

Like many words, *pilgrimage* is one that has been overused to the
point that most people don't really know what it means.
Someone who goes on a pilgrimage is called a "pilgrim." For me,
that word conjures up images of the first Thanksgiving—men
and women with big buckles on their shoes wearing austere,
black and white clothing. No doubt that image is the residue of
my childhood education in New Jersey—but it lingers. My
second- and third-grade teachers notwithstanding, the words *pilgrimage* and *pilgrim* are still used in spiritual contexts and refer to
something very significant. As I shall point out, the notion of
running as pilgrimage can significantly enhance the experience
of a spiritual runner.

PILGRIMAGE IN SPIRITUAL TRADITIONS AROUND THE WORLD

Throughout history, people all over the world have yearned to
make a connection with their spiritual roots—with those places
on this earth most closely associated with what they consider to

be holy. Visiting these places is an expression of faith, a source of blessing, and a quest for healing both spiritual and physical, as well as a source of personal prestige and camaraderie. Members of every major religion participate in pilgrimages. Below are several examples.[2]

- The Buddha spoke of four sites most worthy of pilgrimage for his followers to visit, namely, Lumbini, the Buddha's birthplace; Bodh Gaya, the site where he attained Enlightenment; Benares, where he first preached; and Kusinara, where he passed away.
- In Christianity, pilgrimages were first made to sites connected with the birth, life, crucifixion, and resurrection of Jesus. Pilgrimages also began to be made to Rome and other sites associated with the apostles, the saints, and Christian martyrs, as well as to places where there have been apparitions of the Virgin Mary.
- For Muslims, a pilgrimage to Mecca—called the hajj—is one of the Five Pillars of the faith. It involves visits to many of the sites associated with the Prophet Muhammad and the earliest history of the faith. The hajj should be attempted at least once in a person's lifetime and is required of all able-bodied Muslims who can afford to do so.

Since pilgrimages seem to be a part of all spiritual traditions, let's examine the various elements common to all religious pilgrimages and see whether running can become for us a kind of pilgrimage.

WHAT EXACTLY *IS* A PILGRIMAGE?

Put most simply, a pilgrimage is a journey made to a sacred shrine for the spiritual purposes mentioned above. People who go on pilgrimage may be motivated by emotional or physical pain (in the case of illness), a sense of living a meaningless life, or countless other motives. But a pilgrimage is different from routine trips to holy sites, such as going to church on Sunday or synagogue on Saturday. A pilgrimage involves something deeper and more profound.

But just what sets a pilgrimage apart? Interestingly, scholars have found that pilgrimages from around the world and at all times through history have exemplified three related stages.

SEPARATION FROM THE NORMAL ROUTINE

The first stage of a pilgrimage is the separation from normal routines, separation from the places where the pilgrim lives and works. A pilgrimage is also a separation from routine social relations. The pilgrim is not parent, uncle, or wife; he or she is not a white-collar or a blue-collar worker. The pilgrim leaves all that behind and crosses over to a special place with a new set of relationships, a place where he or she can expect to encounter the Divine.

This separation is both geographical and social and is often symbolized by taking a vow, making a promise, or honoring an obligation to leave home and travel to a holy place. This separation can be symbolized in various ways, such as by taking a new name, cutting the hair, or speaking a new language. Often, pilgrims wear special clothing, which even further separates them from their everyday identity. The pilgrimage begins by a person setting him- or herself apart. Another way that separation takes place is in the location of many—though not all—pilgrimage sites outside the centers of towns and cities. That is, the pilgrimage site is separated from the political and social center of culture.

STANDING ON THE THRESHOLD

In the second stage of a pilgrimage, the pilgrim finds him- or herself on a social and spiritual threshold. A pilgrimage center, or shrine, represents a threshold, like the threshold of a door, and the pilgrim is on that threshold between the everyday world that he or she left behind and the sacred reality. At that place the pilgrim hopes to have a direct experience of the sacred, or supernatural. And it is there that the pilgrim experiences an inward transformation of his or her spirit or personality.

On a pilgrimage a very powerful and distinctive form of social community also emerges. There is an intimate sense of community among the pilgrims, and it is through this feeling of community that a sense of equality develops. This is what the Jewish philosopher Martin Buber called an "I-Thou" awareness.[3] In this I-Thou relationship, you no longer treat other people as if they were objects, you treat them as people—as equals. In our everyday lives, we are used to treating people as objects. This doesn't necessarily mean that we are rude or condescending to others; more often, this is a passive kind of dismissal or disinterest in people. How often do you look at the people you pass on the street—really look them in the eye and engage them? Probably not very often. Most of the people you pass might just as well be objects like the lampposts and mail boxes. On a pilgrimage, this changes. You find yourself among like-minded people who are making a similar quest, and through the journey, you recognize and respond to the humanity in them. You are likely to open up easily, talk to strangers and engage them as people, even as friends. This realization of community can become so profound that you may also experience a compassion for the whole of humanity.

THE JOURNEY HOME

The third stage of the pilgrimage is the journey home. After the pilgrim has made the trip to the pilgrimage site, the pilgrim must return to the society from which he or she came. However, this journey home is the journey of a changed individual. In some cases, the pilgrim can now use a new name indicating his or her new status as someone who has made the pilgrimage. The pilgrim is spiritually renewed and in some cases healed of physical ailments. Forever afterward, the pilgrim becomes a part of that community of pilgrims—both past and present—who have also made the pilgrimage.

Can a Marathon Be a Pilgrimage?

Running can be a form of personal pilgrimage—especially longer, more challenging runs, such as marathons. There are striking similarities between long-distance running and going on a spiritual pilgrimage, suggesting that the spiritual benefits of a more traditional pilgrimage are available to us in the form of a running pilgrimage.

It's important to point out that in order for a marathon (or any run) to be a pilgrimage, you must first establish that you *want* the run to have a spiritual component. Running has the potential to be a pilgrimage, but without a spiritual intention, the marathon will not rise to that level. You can make this intention formally when you choose which marathon you want to run. More and more cities around the world are organizing marathons, so chances are good that there is a marathon near you. Some people, however, have a special attraction to one of the big marathons such as Boston, New York City, Chicago, Minneapolis, or Los Angeles.

Once you have decided that you want the marathon to

> "When we think about what it means to run, what comes to mind are mileage, pace, form, and strength, and when we seek to improve, these are the aspects of training on which we focus. Also essential to running, however, are carbohydrates, protein, iron, and other nutrients. To enjoy the fullest benefit of running, we need to pay attention not only to the outer mechanical aspects of running but to our internal nutritional requirements as well."
> —Claire Kowalchik, *The Complete Book of Running for Women*

be a pilgrimage and know which marathon you will run, the next step is to undergo many months of training. There are many books by capable authors that can help you complete the necessary training for a marathon, which includes a program of diet, cross-training, and daily running. These long hours of running each week will separate you from all your nonrunning friends and family, like the first stage of a pilgrimage (separation from the normal routine). This literally sets you apart, as you spend hours out on the roads and trails, and it also begins to create a separate identity for you. You are no longer identified (simply) as a mother, father, sister, or brother. Instead, you are identified as a marathoner, a runner who averages so many minutes per mile, or something similar.

When the day of the race draws close, additional similarities to a pilgrimage emerge. First comes the geographic separation from your normal habitat. You may need to travel to a different city or go to a hotel in a different part of your own town. Then, the night before the race, there is traditionally a pasta dinner available for all the participants. It is a time to get a good, carbohydrate-rich meal (carbs are very important for the energy you will need for the race) and meet new friends. At dinner, people share stories of other marathons or experiences that prompted them to run this marathon. For many people, this is the real beginning of the marathon experience. They have left home, come to the place of the marathon, checked into a hotel, and now they are meeting their fellow runners and interacting with them as equals and compatriots. The workaday and family identities are put on hold for a time.

The day of the race, you get up early, eat a nutritious but sparse breakfast, put on shorts, T-shirt, socks, and running shoes, and proceed to the starting line of the race. The feeling of community intensifies, and your separation from your routine, everyday society is symbolized by wearing the clothes of a runner. There is a circuslike atmosphere with motivational music and lots of people stretching and warming up. The starter finally gets everybody gathered at the starting line, gives them a brief pep talk, and signals the command to go.

You start running with hundreds, thousands, or tens of thousands of strangers, perhaps striking up a nervous conversation with someone as you get slowly started. Most of these people were strangers to you a few hours earlier, but your collective participation in this event makes them brothers and sisters at heart. The running course, like a pilgrimage site, is separated from the rest of society. Police keep streets blocked off from normal traffic. You are all on the threshold—the threshold of many new emotions and feelings that nonrunners can't understand.

Mile after mile, you are part of this mass of individuals united in that one quest—to complete the 26.2 miles and cross the finish line under your own power. Occasionally, you stop to rehydrate at one of the many tables set up along the road with volunteer workers handing out small cups filled halfway with either water or an energy drink. (Traditional pilgrimages often have free refreshments along the route, too.) From time to time, a runner will have to stop to walk or to stretch out a cramp, and fellow runners will ask if everything is okay or give some word of encouragement. Everyone feels disappointed if someone has to drop out. Runners often "hit the wall" around twenty miles out, but if you get that far and are still running, your spirits will rise, because you only have a little more than six miles to go.

Crossing the finish line is a joy for everyone who does it, and you just might find yourself embracing other runners in congratulations—even people you never saw before. Even though you may not know that person by name, you have much in common with him or her: you are both members of that exclusive group—people who have completed a marathon.

You are very tired, but you are exhilarated. And after a brief rest and refreshment at the finish-line area, you begin your return home, whether by going back to your hotel or driving directly home. From now on, and as long as you live, you are different. You have been *transformed* by it. The marathon mystique is gone; you have conquered the distance (whether you did it in three hours or five) and very well may feel empowered to undertake other difficult tasks or accomplish other great things in your life. You may realize that you can do *anything* you set your mind to. People back home are likely to never view you in quite the same way again.

> "I can't stress enough the need for you to make a commitment to a routine, even though I also believe that you shouldn't feel guilty about missing a workout. If you know that you usually run on Tuesday, Saturday, and Sunday, you focus on those days. Putting off your running for a day or two can start a pattern of procrastination. You miss days, mess up your schedule, and become discouraged. If it's on the calendar, you'll do it. Even when you think you're tired, doing your run energizes you!"
>
> —Kathrine Switzer, *Running and Walking for Women Over 40*

You can experience the benefits of a pilgrimage in the form of a marathon or similar long run any time you choose to put forth the effort. The catch is this: first you must identify what run *can* be a pilgrimage for you—for not all runs are created equal in this way. Discovering what can be your pilgrimage run takes patience and practice. Let's explore this a little further.

THE RUN AS SANCTUARY OR SHRINE

In an earlier chapter we discussed the idea of running as a place, a sanctuary, where you can go to be alone with your thoughts and encounter the sacred reality. In that sense, wherever you take your daily training run is for you a sanctuary much like a church or synagogue is a sanctuary. Such places are set aside for the prayerful gathering of believers.

But a sanctuary, although set apart, is often a place chosen for convenience. The location of a religious group's physical sanctuary may be selected for practical or symbolic reasons—the land was for sale and the congregation could afford to buy it, or it is on high ground, which will enable people to see the sanctuary from far away. In a similar way, your sanctuary run can be any run. It is a run of convenience and symbolic meaning, and can be around your neighborhood, through the park down the street, or on the city streets by the hotel on a business trip.

A pilgrimage site, on the other hand, is not just a sanctuary. It is a *shrine*, and it *presents itself to us*. In that sense, it is not a place chosen for convenience; indeed, in an important sense, it is not a place that *we* have chosen at all. It is the place where important spiritual events happened and are remembered. Or it is a place where people have had visions or experienced miracles. It is a place where the Holy has chosen to break through in a special and unique way. In short, a sanctuary is a place chosen by us; a pilgrimage shrine is a place that, in a way, chooses itself. Just about any run can be a sanctuary, but few of our runs can be true pilgrimages.

LETTING YOUR RUNNING PILGRIMAGE CHOOSE ITSELF

The problem with running as pilgrimage is that you don't choose the pilgrimage shrine, it chooses itself and you must discover it. And that can take time.

To recognize your running pilgrimage, look back through your spiritual running journal. Keeping track of your spiritual experiences while running and your feelings about those runs can help you recognize those places that can serve as your spiritual running pilgrimage. Your journal is something for you to read and draw inspiration from, so by going back to your journal, you will be able to recognize that run or road race that had special meaning for you. For example, if you have ever taken part in a road race for a cause like cancer research because you have a relative who suffered from cancer, that race has the potential of being your pilgrimage. And at that sort of race you will also have a community of people who are pilgrims with you.

Your Spiritual Running Journal

Before you go on to the next chapter, take some time to look back through your spiritual journal, and then write your responses to the following questions.

- Have you ever been on a traditional religious or spiritual pilgrimage? If so, what was that experience like? Can you envision having a similar experience while running?
- On what runs do you find that you consistently have spiritual experiences?
- What do those runs have in common? Location? Time of day? Are they organized road races? If so, are they for a particular charity or organization?
- If the idea of a running pilgrimage appeals to you, how can you turn those more typical runs into a pilgrimage run? Go back to the beginning of this chapter and list what elements set a pilgrimage apart from other experiences. Do any of the runs or races you take part in share these elements? Perhaps that is your pilgrimage.

On Your Next Run

The next time you go for a run, be consciously aware of the ways your run (even a short run) resembles a pilgrimage. Make a special effort to greet other runners you meet. Pay attention to the ways that running actually alters your mood and your perceptions. Recall the runs you have already identified as being potential pilgrimage runs. What marathons or other long runs in your area can you look into? What marathons or other long runs are near places that already have special or spiritual meaning for you—such as a national park or a city that's always held special meaning for you? What steps can you take to make a running pilgrimage there? Can you make a running pilgrimage out of running *to* that place?

● ● ● ●

CHAPTER NINE

SPIRITUAL RUNNING: PREPARING TO PRACTICE

*Don't be concerned if running or exercise
will add years to your life, be concerned
with adding life to your years.*
— *Dr. George Sheehan*[1]

Some years ago a young man took one of my classes. One day in conversation after class, he mentioned that he was a runner. Because I am one of the coaches of the college cross-country team, I encouraged him to try out for the team. I gave him all the standard reasons why he should do this. As a member of the team, I told him, he would get guidance from the coaches, which would enable him to maximize his abilities. Also, as part of a team he would have the encouragement of his teammates to help motivate him to run even at those times when he didn't feel much like running. This would, in turn, add a more enjoyable element to his training.

But the young man was not persuaded, telling me he had been part of athletic teams all his life in high school, junior high, even in grade school. He had had enough of organized sports. The time had come, he told me, to take it easy—take the pressure off himself, run on his own, and just enjoy the sport. What makes this particularly interesting is that he was a very competitive person, and he definitely wanted to excel.

We became friends, and he came to my office often to tell me what road races he was running in. He even entered a few marathons, and I was able to check the results online. His times were okay—but they weren't great. I knew he had the potential to do much better, and in our conversations I could tell that he was growing more and more frustrated with his results.

He graduated college, and his e-mails to me became less and less frequent, until finally they stopped altogether. I found out from some mutual friends that he had continued running for a while, but his job started to get in the way. He gradually ran less and less frequently until he finally seemed to give up the sport altogether.

That was about three years ago, and recently I heard from him again. He told me that he had resumed running. According to him, when he left college he became too busy with his job to keep up his running, but he got back into it when he met some people at work who were members of a running club with a really good coach. They talked him into joining. He even picked up a couple of books on running and was subscribing to *Runner's World* magazine. He was improving as a runner and even was beginning to win some races. Best of all, he was able to avoid the injuries that had plagued him so much when he was running on his own.

After several months, as we reestablished friendship, he was able to share with me his regrets about not joining the cross-country team in college. He now knew that he had wasted a lot of time running on his own, and he realized that all that I had told him was true, and he could have been a lot better runner had he joined the cross-country team.

We are coming near the end of this book, and we have covered a lot of territory, but ultimately this is only an introduction to spirituality and the spiritual art of running. The story I just told you about my young friend is in some ways a good metaphor for the spiritual life—and especially the life of a spiritual runner. The young man was motivated to succeed as a competitive runner, just as you may be motivated to succeed as a spiritual runner, but he found that he could do his best when three factors were present:

1. Proper guidance
2. Adequate support
3. The right attitude

And to succeed as a spiritual runner, you need those same three factors.

WHOEVER YOU ARE, YOU NEED A COACH

As runners—and especially as *spiritual* runners—we are all in a similar situation to that young man. Runners at all levels—from beginners to Olympic champions— all benefit from the guidance of a coach. We can try to get along completely on our own, but the best progress can be made when we have a guide and teacher—or at least the aid of responsible literature written by experts in the field. Each coach has his or her unique approach, strengths, weaknesses, styles of communication, and personality, and some coaches are better able to lead their athletes to success.

The situation is the same when it comes to spirituality. As we began this study, I indicated that more and more people are turning to running to satisfy their spiritual thirst. If you

"Many runners know they should run easy after each hard day. Oregon's Bill Bowerman is credited with this concept.... Walking and other non-pounding cross-training activities will promote recovery better than hitting the couch by generating a gentle circulation of blood, oxygen and nutrients to speed the recovery (and strengthening) process. The late Dr. George Sheehan shifted to running every other day late in his running career. After several years of this, he ran his fastest marathon (3:01) at age 62."
—Jeff Galloway, *Galloway's Book on Running*

attempt to make the spiritual journey completely alone, however, you will be prone to discouragement if your progress is not as quick as you had hoped. This may even lead to your giving up the attempt altogether. Even if you make *some* spiritual progress, you are not likely to reach your full potential. What you need is help. I hope this book has provided you with some assistance, but it is only a beginning. There are other books on spirituality that can provide you with further guidance (I list some books I have found helpful in the Suggestions for Further Reading), and spiritual leaders such as rabbis, priests, or ministers can also serve as spiritual coaches. In order to maximize your spiritual potential, you have to find the "coach" who is right for you.

THE SPIRITUAL EQUIVALENT OF A RUNNING CLUB

The support of a team is essential for the maximum motivation and assistance in difficult circumstances. The recent ESPN movie *Four Minutes* (2005) tells the story of Roger Bannister and his quest to be the first person to run the mile in under four minutes (it is a wonderful movie if you haven't seen it). One of the lessons we can learn from this true story is that Bannister couldn't accomplish his goal without the aid of two good friends, Chris Brasher and Chris Chataway, who served as moral support for him, providing encouragement during training sessions, and, perhaps most important, as "rabbits," taking turns running in front of him and setting the pace, on the day that Bannister ran his record-breaking race.

Just like Bannister or the young man I told you about who eventually joined a running club and got the guidance he needed, we all need spiritual guidance from an experienced and knowledgeable "coach" and the support of a group to grow spiritually.

If you are already a member of a religious organization like a church or synagogue, you surely know the benefits I am referring to here. If you are not affiliated with such a group, I would urge you to consider seeking out a group of spiritually like-minded people who can help you on your journey. Organized religions and other spiritual fellowships provide a source of instruction and a community of people who support and encourage each other. If you had an experience in the past that has led to your dissatisfaction with religious or spiritual groups, perhaps you were simply a member of a group that was wrong for you. With the variety of religious groups and spiritual teachers available today, you are all but certain to find a group with whom you resonate, if you search patiently and intentionally.

If you can't find an organized religious group to your liking, try starting your own spiritual running group. It is not uncommon with running clubs to have, in addition to regular meetings, a special meeting for a long run. These meetings typically meet on Saturday or Sunday morning. The group meets at a specified place, and the members run together for an hour or two. (Usually they will run in smaller groups that form according to their abilities and fitness level.) In my experience, after the run the entire group meets at someone's home for brunch and to discuss the run and other issues related to running. Generally, it is a lot of fun and a welcome social gathering. A similar gathering can be arranged among spiritual runners. Meeting at a specified time on a Saturday or Sunday, a run can be a sanctuary for a group—much like a church or synagogue. Additionally, the run can become a time of worship, prayer, or meditation together with others.

Taking Short Steps, Making Steady Progress

Until recently, I have always hated running up hills. Coach Chris Cameron here at Merrimack College has helped me to get over that. For most runners, hills are only obstacles. Hills take the wind out of your lungs and turn your legs into lead. But I have learned to like hills. They have become a challenge.

Running well on hills requires two important strategies. The first is a positive attitude. You cannot accomplish much if you don't believe that you can. So, having the positive attitude to running up hills is important to doing it well. But second, and perhaps more important, you need to change the way you run—you have to adapt your stride. You can't run hills well if you use the same stride you use on flat roads. You must run with shorter strides, leaning forward slightly, looking at the path about five or six feet in front of you. Although you don't go very far with each stride, you do make steady progress, which is most important.

To make progress as a spiritual runner is at times like running up a hill. It is essential for you to have the right attitude. You have to believe that what you are doing is making you a more spiritual person, and part of the right attitude is having the right knowledge, knowing the truth. But also important is knowing that you have to make adjustments. Progress will be slow at times, but if you keep at it, you will advance.

> "Running uphill doesn't require working all that much harder than on the flats. Just slow down to maintain the same effort level or heart rate that you were doing beforehand. You should also shorten your stride so that you're not straining too hard on each toe-off, but this will probably feel natural enough that you won't have to think about it.... Running downhill is trickier. Most runners tend to "put on the brakes" by deliberately overstriding and using their quadriceps muscles to hold themselves back. This is tiring and is jarring on the knees. If the slope isn't too extreme, try leaning into it a bit, increasing your leg speed (the number of steps you make per minute) to keep from falling on your face. Be particularly careful about not reaching out."
> —Alberto Salazar, *Alberto Salazar's Guide to Running: A Champion's Revolutionary Program to Revitalize Your Fitness*

ENTHUSIASM WITHOUT CONTENT

Enthusiasm is normally a good thing to have. I think we are all impressed by people who are enthusiastic about what they do—whatever that is. But enthusiasm must also be linked to a certain amount of knowledge—especially in spirituality—otherwise, it turns into fanaticism or superstition. I heard a story recently about a student from a big university who was away from campus when he heard news of a big protest march at his school. All excited, he said, "Oh, I'm so sorry I missed it! If I were there, I would have been in it ... what's it about, anyway?" He had an eagerness and a passion for action, but it was without knowledge. As one social commentator has remarked, "Many have zeal without knowledge, enthusiasm without enlightenment. In more modern jargon, they are keen but clueless."[2]

Enthusiasm in running is helpful, too. But along with that enthusiasm must come a sufficient content. One of my most embarrassing moments in running came as a high school junior. On the day of a track meet, I was told by my track coach that I would not be running the 440-yard run as I normally did. Instead, I was going to run the mile. When the race started, I was fast off the starting line—too fast. I was enthusiastic, but I didn't know enough about the race to know that I needed to pace myself better. Although I led for most of the race, I suddenly ran out of steam, fell behind, and in the end I came in third place. That was a big lesson for me. I found out that my enthusiasm for running had to be tempered with the proper knowledge.

To know the truth about something can really be a liberating experience. That sentiment has been expressed many times and in many ways, but perhaps the most famous expression of that thought is in the following words: "You will know the truth and the truth shall make you free."[3] It is used so much because it expresses something that we all can agree with. Good feelings will not free us; good intentions will not free us. Only knowledge of the truth will free us—free us from ignorance and free us to be our best.

I have talked about running and freedom at a number of places throughout this book. I have said that running is an expression of our natural desire, as human beings, to be free. By ourselves, we don't always know what that desire for freedom is all about, but as runners, we know that running helps us express that desire.

Further, as a runner I feel like I have something special. Many people have tried to express this, but for me the person who said it best was George Sheehan when he wrote, "The true runner is a very fortunate person. He has found something in him that is just perfect."[4] Having made contact with that part of myself, the spiritual quest—which is the endeavor to find who I am and be truly at home with myself, to establish a healthy relationship with others, and to have a healthy relationship with God—is a natural outcome. And all the aspects of true spirituality that I outlined at the beginning of this book are related, for as Thomas Merton once observed, "We cannot be at peace with others because we are not at peace with ourselves, and we are not at peace with ourselves because we are not at peace with God."[5]

Your Spiritual Running Journal

For the final spiritual running journal exercise (but, by all means, continue journaling after you finish the book!), go back to the quotations that begin each of the chapters. Take them one at a time and write down your reactions and responses to each one. Which ones resonate with you? Which ones don't? It may be that as your spiritual running progresses, those quotations that hold no meaning for you now will at a later time.

On Your Next Run

Before you go out for a run, turn to the first two quotations with which this book began—the quotations by

Roger Bannister and C. S. Lewis. The next time you go for a run, meditate on one of them and then write down your reflections in your journal. On your subsequent run, do the same with the other quotation. Together, I believe, these quotations express the essence of spiritual running.

A FINAL WORD

If you have read this book carefully and have tried to engage in the practice of spiritual running as I have described it, you have begun to take part in an ancient spiritual discipline that has spanned cultures around the globe. You have become a spiritual brother or sister to the ancient Olympic athletes of Greece, the Marathon Monks of Japan, and countless others. Your methods may be different, your ability and attire may be different, but you have embarked on a similar spiritual quest. The Hebrew prophet Jeremiah expresses a truth about God that I believe is near to the heart of them all when he wrote, "If you seek me, you will find me, when you seek for me with all your heart" (Jer. 29:13).

Finally, if you have found in the pages of this book something you like or something you find helpful, I am overjoyed. To you, I feel a kinship more than you will ever know.

●　●　●　●

ACKNOWLEDGMENTS

This book was not written alone. Although there is some truth to the idea of "the loneliness of the long-distance runner," running also creates community, and I am very lucky to be part of a large community of runners and friends who have all, in their own ways, contributed to this book. Thank you for your support and encouragement, but especially for your love and friendship. I would like to draw attention to just a few people who have left their mark on me and also on this book.

First, I would like to thank my sister, Susan, and her husband, Bob Rogers, for reading through earlier versions of this book and for making many helpful comments. You guys are the greatest!

Thanks to my brother Charley, who read a few chapters and made numerous helpful stylistic comments.

Also, thanks to the members of the Merrimack College cross-country teams, both past and present, and especially our head coach, Chris Cameron. Chris, it has been a blast running with you! Thanks for the memories and for your friendship.

Thanks to Mike and Marianne Gray and Fernando Braz—friends and fellow runners. It is people like you who keep me inspired to run ... *and* to enjoy it.

Thanks to my son, Alex. Those were really "special times" running on the Bedford bike path, and I hope you had *half* as much fun as I did.

Thanks to the members of the "Spirituality of Running" classes at Merrimack College and especially to Pete Challoner. Thanks, Pete; your participation, engagement with the subject matter, and continued friendship are greatly appreciated.

Special thanks to my editor at SkyLight Paths, Mark Ogilbee, for inviting me to write this book. You have been a constant help in making it more readable. I owe you a lot.

Most of all, I want to thank my wife, Nancy, the love of my life, for putting up with me during these months of writing this book (how many times did I watch that Roger Bannister clip?). You have been my constant support, not only in running but also in life.

Finally, this book is dedicated to my father, Herbert Ralph Kay, who, with my brothers, Dave, Dan, and Charley, helped and inspired me in my early years of running and who, with my mother, Adrianna Wilhelmina Spruit, first set me on the spiritual path.

NOTES

INTRODUCTION

1. John L. Parker Jr., *Once a Runner* (Tallahassee, FL: Cedarwinds Publishing, 1978, 1990).

2. John Jerome, *The Elements of Effort: Reflections on the Art and Science of Running* (New York: Breakaway Books, 1997), 14.

3. Years later Ron Delaney described what he was thinking and feeling those first few moments after he won the Olympic gold medal: "As I crossed the line, I threw my arms up in joy, and the first thing I remember thinking is 'I just can't believe it.' My second instinct was to kneel down and give a prayer of thanksgiving." Steve Landells, "When Irish (and 'Nova) Eyes Smiled. Ron Delany's Olympic Triumph in 1956 Cemented Ties Between a University and a Country," *The Philadelphia Inquirer*, December 1, 2006.

4. In college Jeff Galloway was All-American in cross-country and track and made the 1972 Olympic team for the 10,000-meter run. He set the American record for the 10-mile run and was a member of several United States national track and field teams.

5. In addition to the books I have used as sources for these quotations and the books on running listed in the Suggestions for Further Reading at the end of this book, some of the most famous quotations on running have been gathered together by Mark Will-Weber in *The Quotable Runner* (New York: Breakaway Books, 1995).

CHAPTER 1

1. This quotation was used by Roger Bannister at the start of his autobiography *The First Four Minutes* (London: Putnam & Sons Ltd., 1955). Although neither of us is using the passage in its proper

historical sense, it does make for a nice starting point for both books. For me, I wish to express the fact that I have a "vision" of what running can be for some people, namely, a passageway into a real and vital spiritual experience, and this book is an attempt to write my ideas in as clear a fashion as possible so that other people can experience this, too.

2. Jim Fixx, *The Complete Book of Running* (New York: Random House, 1977).

3. *Jim Fixx's Second Book of Running* (New York: Random House, 1984).

4. George Sheehan, *Running and Being: The Total Experience* (New York: Simon and Schuster, 1978).

5. Amby Burfoot won the Boston Marathon in 1968 and is currently senior editor for *Runner's World* magazine. He has written some of the best books on running and how to get started in fitness running.

6. The term *fast-food nation* is borrowed from the title of a book by Eric Schlosser, *Fast Food Nation* (New York: Harper Perennial, 2005).

7. Ibid., 19.

8. John Haldane, *An Intelligent Person's Guide to Religion* (London: Duckworth, 2003), 133.

9. *Time* magazine, cover story, April 8, 1966, 82–87.

10. Robert N. Bellah, *Habits of the Heart* (Berkeley and Los Angeles: University of California Press, 1985).

11. Bellah, *Habits of the Heart*, 221.

12. Bannister, *The First Four Minutes*, 11–12.

13. C. S. Lewis, *Surprised by Joy* (New York: Harcourt, Brace & World, 1955), 220.

14. Although not a world-class runner himself, John "The Penguin" Bingham has inspired many thousands of men and women to take up fitness running through his best-selling books *No Need for Speed* and *The Courage to Start* and through his monthly column for *Runner's World* magazine.

15. Jeff Galloway, "The Five Stages of a Runner," in *Galloway's Book on Running*, 2nd ed. (Bolinas, CA: Shelter Publications, 2002), 12–19.

CHAPTER 2

1. F. F. Bruce, *Paul: Apostle of the Heart Set Free* (Grand Rapids, MI: William B. Eerdmans, 1977), 74–75.

2. Karen Armstrong, *Muhammad: A Biography of the Prophet* (San Francisco: HarperCollins, 1992), 82–83.

3. Ian Barbour, *Religion in an Age of Science* (San Francisco: Harper & Row, 1990), 4–8.

4. Bernd Heinrich, "Ancient Runners and Us," in *Why We Run: A Natural History* (New York: HarperCollins, 2001), 7–12.

5. Peter L. Berger, *A Rumor of Angels: Modern Society and the Rediscovery of the Supernatural* (Garden City, NY: Doubleday, 1969), 65ff.

6. C. S. Lewis, *Mere Christianity* (New York: Macmillan, 1952), 106.

7. Many popular news magazines have recently featured articles on spirituality. One noteworthy example is "Spirituality in America," *Newsweek*, September 5, 2005.

8. Brother Lawrence, *The Practice of the Presence of God, with Spiritual Maxims* (Boston: Shambhala Publications, 2005), 75.

9. Nigel Spivey, *The Ancient Olympics: A History* (Oxford: Oxford University Press, 2004), 111–17.

10. William K. Guthrie, *The Greeks and Their Gods* (Boston: Beacon, 1971).

11. M. I. Finley and H. W. Pleket, *The Olympic Games: The First Thousand Years* (New York: Dover, 2005).

12. John Stevens, *The Marathon Monks of Mount Hiei* (Boston: Shambhala, 1988).

13. "On the Road Again," *Runner's World*, October 2006, 66–74.

14. Alexandra David-Néel, *Magic and Mystery in Tibet* (New York: Claude Kendall, 1932).

15. Ibid., 202–203.

16. Alberto Salazar was the winner of the Boston Marathon and three consecutive New York City Marathons in the early 1980s. He held six U.S. records and one world record for running.

CHAPTER 3

1. Wayne Lee, *To Rise from Earth* (Facts on File, 1996).

2. *Babylonian Talmud*, Hul. 60a.

3. Kathrine Switzer was the first woman to officially enter and run the Boston Marathon. She won the New York City Marathon in 1974 and has worked hard to establish opportunities for women in running.

4. The philosopher Ludwig Wittgenstein includes a discussion of this in his *Philosophical Investigations*, 3rd ed., trans. G. E. M. Anscombe (Oxford: Basil Blackwell Publishing, 1953, 1958), 193–208.

5. Thomas Merton, *New Seeds of Contemplation* (Boston: Shambhala, 2003), 1.

6. Claire Kowalchik, a veteran of many marathons and other road races, is the former managing editor for *Runner's World* magazine and has written for numerous sports and fitness publications.

7. Blaise Pascal, *Pensées*, no. 430, ed. Brunschvicg (New York: E. P. Dutton, 1932), 118.

CHAPTER 4

1. This quotation is the title of one of George Sheehan's essays and can be found at the following website: www.georgesheehan.com/essays/essay46.html.

2. Henri J. M. Nouwen, *The Genesee Diary: Report from a Trappist Monastery* (Garden City, NY: Doubleday, 1976).

3. This account and the two quotations are taken from a paper written by one of my students for the course I teach, "The Spirituality of Running," and is used by permission.

4. Alfred North Whitehead, *Religion in the Making* (Cambridge: Cambridge University Press, 1927), 6.

5. Abraham Joshua Heschel, *Man's Quest for God: Studies in Prayer and Symbolism* (New York: Charles Scribner's Sons, 1954), xiv.

6. Richard B. Pilgrim, "Ritual," in *Introduction to the Study of Religion*, ed. T. William Hall (San Francisco: Harper & Row, 1978), 65.

7. Quoted in Bob Abernethy and William Bole, *The Life of Meaning: Reflections on Faith, Doubt, and Repairing the World* (New York: Seven Stories Press, 2007), 151–52.

8. Amby Burfoot, *The Runner's Guide to the Meaning of Life: What 35 Years of Running Has Taught Me about Winning, Losing, Happiness, Humility, and the Human Heart* (Emmaus, PA: Rodale, 2000), 59.

9. Alberto Salazar, *Alberto Salazar's Guide to Running: A Champion's Revolutionary Program to Revitalize Your Fitness* (New York: McGraw-Hill, 2001), 82.

10. Sheehan, *Running and Being*, 229.

CHAPTER 5

1. Victor Hugo, *Les Miserables*, trans. Norman Denny (London: Penguin, 1982), 804.

2. The poet was the great German philosopher and poet Novalis (1772–1801), and this quotation is from Friedrich Heiler's classic study, *Prayer: A Study in the History and Psychology of Religion* (Oxford: Oxford University Press, 1932), xiii.

3. C. S. Lewis, *God in the Dock: Essays on Theology and Ethics* (Grand Rapids, MI: William B. Eerdmans, 1971), 176.

4. Paul Ulasien, *The Corporate Rat Race: The Rats Are Winning: A Game Plan for Surviving and Thriving in Corporate America* (Frederick, MD: PublishAmerica, 2006).

5. I am indebted to John Macquarrie for the heading of this section and for his clarification of the notion of prayer. John Macquarrie, "Prayer as Thinking," *Paths in Spirituality* (New York: Morehouse Group, 1993), 25–39.

6. Dag Hammarskjöld, *Markings* (New York: Knopf, 1964), 122.

7. Much of the material on the techniques for prayer around the world was taken from Geoffrey Parrinder, *Worship in the World's Religions* (London: Faber & Faber, 1961).

8. Kristen Armstrong, "Buddy System: Counting Your Blessings Can Carry You Through 26.2," *Runner's World*, July 2006, 68.

9. Maureen McNellis and Karen Schulte, "The Runner's Prayer," in *Day By Day: The Notre Dame Prayerbook for Students*, eds. Thomas McNally and William G. Storey (Notre Dame, IN: Ave Maria Press, 2004), 71.

CHAPTER 6

1. Bhagavad Gita, xviii, 53.

2. *The Sayings of Muhammad*, comp. Sir Abdullah al-Mamun Suhrawardy (New York: Citadel Press, 2000), 94.

3. Paul Reps and Nyogen Senzaki, eds. *Zen Flesh, Zen Bones: A Collection of Zen and Pre-Zen Writings,* comp. (Rutland, VT: Charles E. Tuttle, 1957), 48.

4. Henri J. M. Nouwen, *Reaching Out: The Three Movements of the Spiritual Life* (Garden City, NY: Doubleday, 1975), 36.

5. Paul T. Harris, "Silent Teaching: The Life of Dom John Main," *Spirituality Today* 40, no. 4 (Winter 1988): 320–32.

6. Henri J. M. Nouwen with Michael J. Christensen and Rebecca J. Laird, *Spiritual Direction: Wisdom for the Long Walk of Faith* (New York: HarperCollins, 2006), 91.

7. Henri J. M. Nouwen, *Reaching Out*, 50.

8. Sheehan, *Running and Being*, 225.

9. Dietrich Bonhoeffer, *Life Together* (New York: Harper & Row, 1954), 83.

CHAPTER 7

1. Elizabeth Barrett Browning, "Aurora Leigh," in *The Complete Poetical Works of Elizabeth Barrett Browning*, bk. vii (Boston: Houghton Mifflin, 1900), 372.

2. Isaac Newton, quoted by Sir David Brewster in *Memoirs of the Life, Writings, and Discoveries of Sir Isaac Newton*, vol. II (Edinburgh: Thomas Constable, 1855), 407.

3. St. Augustine, *Confessions*, I, 1, i.

4. As quoted in Van A. Harvey, *A Handbook of Theological Terms* (New York: Macmillan, 1964), 211.

5. Paul Tillich, *Biblical Religion and the Search for Ultimate Reality* (Chicago: University of Chicago Press, 1955), 22–23.

6. John Macquarrie, *A Guide to the Sacraments* (New York: Continuum, 1999), 1. Much of what I have to say in this chapter is deeply indebted to this book.

7. Joseph Maros, *Doors to the Sacred* (Garden City, NY: Doubleday, 1981).

8. Amby Burfoot, *The Runner's Guide to the Meaning of Life* (New York: St. Martin's Press, 2000), 79.

9. Ibid., 80.

10. For a very good discussion of the runner's high—what it is and what it isn't—see Amby Burfoot's article, "Is There Really a Runner's High?" *Runner's World*, June 2004, 59–61.

11. Alexander Solzhenitsyn, *A World Split Apart* (New York: Harper & Row, 1978).

12. In saying this, I am borrowing the title of one of John Hick's books, *God Has Many Names* (New York: Macmillan, 1980).

13. Edward Hastings, "Been Plucking Blackberries for Too Long," *Spirituality* 10, no. 3 (2004): 160–166.

CHAPTER 8

1. Frederick Buechner, *Beyond Words: Daily Readings in the ABC's of Faith* (San Francisco: HarperCollins, 2004), 340.

2. Simon Coleman and John Elsner, *Pilgrimage: Past and Present in the World Religions*, British Museum Paperbacks (Cambridge, MA: Harvard University Press, 1997).

3. Martin Buber, *I and Thou* (Edinburgh: T. & T. Clark, 1970).

CHAPTER 9

1. This is a famous saying attributed to George Sheehan but its source is unknown.

2. John Stott, *Your Mind Matters: The Place of the Mind in the Christian Life* (Downers Grove, IL: InterVarsity Press, 2007), 7.

3. John 8:32.

4. Mark Will-Weber, ed., *The Quotable Runner* (New York: Breakaway Books, 1995).

5. Thomas Merton, *The Living Bread* (New York: Farrar, Straus and Cudahy, 1956), xiii.

SUGGESTIONS FOR FURTHER READING

RUNNING

GENERAL BOOKS

Battista, Garth, ed., *How Running Changed My Life: True Stories of the Power of Running.* Halcottsville, NY: Breakaway Books, 2002.

A very interesting collection of real stories by a wide variety of people from different walks of life (and some from other parts of the world) with personal accounts of how running has had an impact—sometimes profound—on their lives, demonstrating that running can be helpful in more ways than just getting in shape.

————. *The Runner's Literary Companion: Great Stories and Poems about Running.* Halcottsville, NY: Breakaway Books, 1994.

Another interesting collection by Battista, this time of fictional stories about running. They are mostly just fun to read, but these stories can be motivational as well.

Bingham, John. *No Need for Speed.* Emmaus, PA: Rodale, 2002.

John "The Penguin" Bingham writes a column for *Runner's World* magazine. An enjoyable read, this book is full of witty and practical insights on running that can be of value to runners at all levels.

Burfoot, Amby. *The Runner's Guide to the Meaning of Life: What 35 Years of Running Have Taught Me about Winning, Losing, Happiness, Humility, and the Human Heart.* Emmaus, PA: Rodale Books/ Daybreak Books, 2000.

Burfoot is the 1968 winner of the Boston Marathon. He has written and edited numerous books on running and is one of the best writers for *Runner's World* magazine—of which he is a senior editor. This book is not on the spirituality of running per se, but it does describe the pleasures of running, with a lot of personal tidbits from this amazing runner. This book can be a source of motivation and inspiration for anyone who runs.

Fee, Earl. *The Complete Guide to Running: How to Be a Champion from 9 to 90.* Oxford: Meyer and Meyer Sport, 2005.

This is one of the most readable, attractive, and comprehensive guides to all aspects of the sport of running available in any language. It is also reasonably priced.

Galloway, Jeff. *Galloway's Book on Running*, 2nd ed. Bolinas, CA: Shelter Publications, 2002.

Written by Olympian Jeff Galloway (1972 Munich Olympics, 10,000 meters), this is one of my favorite how-to books on running. It starts with two particularly helpful chapters for spiritual runners—one on the "running revolution," which gives a thumbnail sketch of how running has become popular in our society, and another on "the five stages of a runner," which is a useful guide to help you see where you are as a runner and to see where you want to be (and even what you may wish to avoid!). The rest of the book is first-rate as well.

————. *Running: Getting Started.* Oxford: Meyer and Meyer Sport, 2006.

————. *Running Until You're 100.* Oxford: Meyer and Meyer Sport, 2007.

Heinrich, Bernd. *Why We Run: A Natural History.* New York: HarperCollins, 2001.

Written by a biologist who is also a great runner, this book is filled with lots of fascinating biological stories about why certain things are important to us as runners, presented in the form of "lessons from the animals." The chapters on biology (which are interesting in themselves) are interspersed with stories from his own life and running career.

Higdon, Hal. *How to Train.* Emmaus, PA: Rodale, 1997.

This is a great general book on running with many helpful tips on running by one of America's best running trainers.

Parker, John L. *Once a Runner.* Tallahassee, FL: Cedarwinds Publishing, 1978, 1990.

In my opinion, *Once a Runner* is the greatest novel written about running. It is more geared to track running, and gives a really accurate feel for what elite runners go through, both physically and mentally. This is a classic!

WOMEN AND RUNNING

Kowalchik, Claire. *The Complete Book of Running for Women.* New York: Pocket Books, 1999.

Murphy, Frank. *The Silence of Great Distance: Women Running Long.* Windsprint Press, 2000.

This book tells the story of women's athletics, with a special focus on long-distance running.

Reti, Irene, and Bettianne Shoney Sien. *Women Runners: Stories of Transformation.* New York: Breakaway Books, 2001.

This is a collection of stories about running and runners written by women for women.

Samuelson, Joan Benoit, and Gloria Averbuch. *Joan Samuelson's Running for Women.* Emmaus, PA: Rodale Press, 1995.

Written by a two-time Boston Marathon winner and gold medalist at the 1984 Olympic Games, this is an all-around book on running for women runners of all levels.

Scott, Dagny. *Runner's World Complete Book of Women's Running.* Emmaus, PA: Rodale, 2000.

Switzer, Kathrine. *Running and Walking for Women Over 40.* New York: St. Martin's, 1998.

Switzer broke the gender barrier in 1967 by being the first woman to run in the Boston Marathon with a race number, and in 1974 she won the New York City Marathon. This book is more than just a guide to running for women over forty—it contains much valuable and inspiring information for women runners of any age.

SPIRITUALITY OF SPORTS AND OF RUNNING

Cooper, Andrew. *Playing in the Zone: Exploring the Spiritual Dimensions of Sports.* Boston: Shambhala, 1998.

Although I don't always agree with Cooper, this is one of the only books out there on the spirituality of sports! It is quite well written and has many good insights.

Joslin, Roger D. *Running the Spiritual Path: A Runner's Guide to Breathing, Meditating, and Exploring the Prayerful Dimension of the Sport.* New York: St. Martin's Press, 2003.

This is a pioneering work in the field of spirituality and running.

Novak, Michael. *Joy of Sports: Endzones, Bases, Baskets, Balls, and the Consecration of the American Spirit*, rev. ed. Lanham, MD: Madison Books, 1993.

Written by a very well-known social analyst, this highly informative and provocative book explores the relationship Americans have with their sports. It is not limited to running, nor is it limited to those who participate in sports, but includes a lot about the sports fan as well. Useful for anyone concerned with the spirituality of sports.

SPIRITUALITY

Armstrong, Kristin. *Happily Ever After: Walking with Peace and Courage through a Year of Divorce.* New York: Faith Words, 2007.

Kristin Armstrong is a writer for *Runner's World* magazine and a good runner herself. She is also former wife of Lance Armstrong, and in this devotional book, she has written 365 brief meditative pieces, intended to help those who are going through similar difficulties. They are nice and short and can be read with great value even if you have not gone through a divorce.

Cleman, Simon, and John Elsner. *Pilgrimage: Past and Present in the World Religions.* Cambridge, MA: Harvard University Press, 1997.

Accompanied by great illustrations, this book tells the story of religious pilgrimages as they are practiced in a variety of religions around the world.

Cooper, David A. *Heart of Stillness: A Complete Guide to Learning the Art of Meditation.* Woodstock, VT: SkyLight Paths, 1999.

This is a very good introduction and guide to the practice of meditation for people of all faiths. A great companion to chapter 6 of the present work.

Cunningham, Lawrence S., and Keith J. Egan. *Christian Spirituality: Themes from the Tradition.* New York: Paulist Press, 1996.

This is one of the standard general introductions to Christian spirituality, although it emphasizes the Roman Catholic tradition. It covers many of the same themes as the present book (but without the running parts).

Foster, Richard J., and Emilie Griffin, eds. *Spiritual Classics: Selected Readings for Individuals and Groups on the Twelve Spiritual Disciplines.* New York: HarperCollins, 2000.

This book includes dozens of selections from St. Augustine to Martin Luther King Jr., with meditations, discussion questions, and exercises, to assist in spiritual growth.

Gattuso, John, ed. *Talking to God: Portrait of a World at Prayer.* Milford, NJ: Stone Creek Publications, 2006.

A collection of fifteen essays by prominent scholars and religious leaders like the Dalai Lama, Thich Nhat Hanh, Thomas Merton, Desmond Tutu, and Karen Armstrong, this book explores the universal significance of prayer. Very inspiring reading, accompanied by more than one hundred photographs taken in over fifty countries.

Keen, Sam. *Hymns to an Unknown God: Awakening the Spirit in Everyday Life.* New York: Bantam Books, 1994.

This is a very provocative guide to spirituality by a best-selling author. When read with an open mind, there is a lot to learn from this great writer.

Kushner, Lawrence. *Jewish Spirituality: A Brief Introduction for Christians.* Woodstock, VT: Jewish Lights Publishing, 2001.

A really good book on Jewish spirituality by a very popular writer. Highly recommended.

Lionberger, John. *Renewal in the Wilderness: A Spiritual Guide to Connecting with God in the Natural World.* Woodstock, VT: SkyLight Paths, 2007.

This book details much of what I have been discussing about seeing God in chapter 3.

Montaldo, Jonathan, ed. *A Year with Thomas Merton: Daily Meditations from His Journal.* San Francisco: HarperSanFrancisco, 2004.

These selections from the writings of Thomas Merton make a convenient meditation for reading before your spiritual runs.

Muldoon, Tim. *The Ignatian Workout: Daily Spiritual Exercises for a Healthy Faith.* Chicago: Loyola Press, 2004.

This is a very creative book, again written from a Roman Catholic perspective, and using sports as a metaphor for religious spirituality. Very helpful and practical, but not specifically geared to running.

Nouwen, Henri. *Bread for the Journey: A Daybook of Wisdom and Faith*. San Francisco: HarperCollins, 1997.

    Short meditations for every day of the year by one of the great writers on spirituality.

Renard, John. *Seven Doors to Islam: Spirituality and the Religious Life of Muslims*. Berkeley: University of California Press, 1996.

    A very good book on Muslim spirituality. This book is not what I would call easy reading, however.

Reps, Paul, and Nyogen Senzaki, eds. *Zen Flesh, Zen Bones: A Collection of Zen and Pre-Zen Writings*. Rutland, VT, and Tokyo: Charles E. Tuttle, 1957.

    This is a collection of more than one hundred beautiful and inspiring stories from the primary sources of Zen Buddhism.

Speerstra, Karen, ed. *Divine Sparks: Collected Wisdom of the Heart*. Sandpoint, ID: Morning Light Press, 2005.

    This is a collection of sayings from many different philosophies and spiritual traditions, organized alphabetically according to topics.

Strand, Clark. *Meditation without Gurus: A Guide to the Heart of Practice*. Woodstock, VT: SkyLight Paths Publishing, 2003.

    Written by a former Buddhist monk, this book is a very enjoyable introduction to meditation.

Wright, N. T. *Simply Christian: Why Christianity Makes Sense*. San Francisco: HarperSanFrancisco, 2006.

    Absolutely the best thing out there. This recent introduction to Christianity is a joy to read. It is equally helpful to those who know nothing about the subject as well as those who are lifelong Christians. A bit challenging here and there, but it is definitely worth the time and effort. Particularly helpful are the early chapters exploring the basis of spirituality in human beings.

JOURNALING

Although there is a lot of literature on journal writing, the following two books are the best on this activity for religious or spiritually minded people.

Budd, Luann. *Journal Keeping: Writing for Spiritual Growth*. Downers Grove, IL: InterVarsity Press, 2002.

Klug, Ron. *How to Keep a Spiritual Journal: A Guide to Journal Keeping for Inner Growth and Personal Discovery*, rev. ed. Minneapolis, MN: Augsburg/Fortress Publishers, 2002.

Meditation / Prayer

Prayers to an Evolutionary God
by William Cleary; Afterword by Diarmuid O'Murchu

How is it possible to pray when God is dislocated from heaven, dispersed all around us, and more of a creative force than an all-knowing father? Inspired by the spiritual and scientific teachings of Diarmuid O'Murchu and Teilhard de Chardin, Cleary reveals that religion and science can be combined to create an expanding view of the universe—an evolutionary faith.

6 x 9, 208 pp, HC, 978-1-59473-006-1 **$21.99**

Psalms: A Spiritual Commentary
by M. Basil Pennington, OCSO; Illustrations by Phillip Ratner

Showing how the Psalms give profound and candid expression to both our highest aspirations and our deepest pain, the late, highly respected Cistercian Abbot M. Basil Pennington shares his reflections on some of the most beloved passages from the Bible's most widely read book.

6 x 9, 176 pp, HC, 24 full-page b/w illus., 978-1-59473-141-9 **$19.99**

The Song of Songs: A Spiritual Commentary
by M. Basil Pennington, OCSO; Illustrations by Phillip Ratner

Join the late M. Basil Pennington as he ruminates on the Bible's most challenging mystical text. Follow a path into the Songs that weaves through his inspired words and the evocative drawings of Jewish artist Phillip Ratner—a path that reveals your own humanity and leads to the deepest delight of your soul.

6 x 9, 160 pp, HC, 14 b/w illus., 978-1-59473-004-7 **$19.99**

Women of Color Pray: Voices of Strength, Faith, Healing, Hope and Courage
Edited and with Introductions by Christal M. Jackson

Through these prayers, poetry, lyrics, meditations and affirmations, you will share in the strong and undeniable connection women of color share with God. It will challenge you to explore new ways of prayerful expression.

5 x 7¼, 208 pp, Quality PB, 978-1-59473-077-1 **$15.99**

The Art of Public Prayer: Not for Clergy Only
by Lawrence A. Hoffman

An ecumenical resource for all people looking to change hardened worship patterns.

6 x 9, 288 pp, Quality PB, 978-1-893361-06-5 **$18.99**

Finding Grace at the Center, 3rd Ed.: The Beginning of Centering Prayer
by M. Basil Pennington, OCSO, Thomas Keating, OCSO, and Thomas E. Clarke, SJ
Foreword by Rev. Cynthia Bourgeault, PhD

5 x 7¼, 128 pp, Quality PB, 978-1-59473-182-2 **$12.99**

A Heart of Stillness: A Complete Guide to Learning the Art of Meditation
by David A. Cooper 5½ x 8½, 272 pp, Quality PB, 978-1-893361-03-4 **$16.95**

Meditation without Gurus: A Guide to the Heart of Practice
by Clark Strand 5½ x 8½, 192 pp, Quality PB, 978-1-893361-93-5 **$16.95**

Praying with Our Hands: 21 Practices of Embodied Prayer from the World's Spiritual Traditions
by Jon M. Sweeney; Photographs by Jennifer J. Wilson; Foreword by Mother Tessa Bielecki; Afterword by Taitetsu Unno, PhD

8 x 8, 96 pp, 22 duotone photos, Quality PB, 978-1-893361-16-4 **$16.95**

Silence, Simplicity & Solitude: A Complete Guide to Spiritual Retreat at Home
by David A. Cooper 5½ x 8½, 336 pp, Quality PB, 978-1-893361-04-1 **$16.95**

Three Gates to Meditation Practice: A Personal Journey into Sufism, Buddhism, and Judaism
by David A. Cooper 5½ x 8½, 240 pp, Quality PB, 978-1-893361-22-5 **$16.95**

Women Pray: Voices through the Ages, from Many Faiths, Cultures and Traditions
Edited and with Introductions by Monica Furlong

5 x 7¼, 256 pp, Quality PB, 978-1-59473-071-9 **$15.99**
Deluxe HC with ribbon marker, 978-1-893361-25-6 **$19.99**

Spirituality

Jewish Spirituality: A Brief Introduction for Christians   by *Lawrence Kushner*
5½ x 8½, 112 pp, Quality PB, 978-1-58023-150-3 **$12.95** *(a Jewish Lights book)*

Journeys of Simplicity: Traveling Light with Thomas Merton, Bashō, Edward Abbey, Annie Dillard & Others by *Philip Harnden* 5 x 7¼, 144 pp, Quality PB, 978-1-59473-181-5 **$12.99**
128 pp, HC, 978-1-893361-76-8 **$16.95**

Keeping Spiritual Balance As We Grow Older: More than 65 Creative Ways to Use Purpose, Prayer, and the Power of Spirit to Build a Meaningful Retirement
by *Molly and Bernie Srode* 8 x 8, 224 pp, Quality PB, 978-1-59473-042-9 **$16.99**

The Monks of Mount Athos: A Western Monk's Extraordinary Spiritual Journey on Eastern Holy Ground by *M. Basil Pennington, ocso; Foreword by Archimandrite Dionysios*
6 x 9, 256 pp, 10+ b/w line drawings, Quality PB, 978-1-893361-78-2 **$18.95**

One God Clapping: The Spiritual Path of a Zen Rabbi by *Alan Lew with Sherrill Jaffe*
5½ x 8½, 336 pp, Quality PB, 978-1-58023-115-2 **$16.95** *(a Jewish Lights book)*

Prayer for People Who Think Too Much: A Guide to Everyday, Anywhere Prayer from the World's Faith Traditions by *Mitch Finley*
5½ x 8½, 224 pp, Quality PB, 978-1-893361-21-8 **$16.99**; HC, 978-1-893361-00-3 **$21.95**

Show Me Your Way: The Complete Guide to Exploring Interfaith Spiritual Direction
by *Howard A. Addison*   5½ x 8½, 240 pp, Quality PB, 978-1-893361-41-6 **$16.95**

Spirituality 101: The Indispensable Guide to Keeping—or Finding—Your Spiritual Life on Campus by *Harriet L. Schwartz, with contributions from college students at nearly thirty campuses across the United States* 6 x 9, 272 pp, Quality PB, 978-1-59473-000-9 **$16.99**

Spiritually Incorrect: Finding God in All the Wrong Places by *Dan Wakefield; Illus. by Marian DelVecchio* 5½ x 8½, 192 pp, b/w illus., Quality PB, 978-1-59473-137-2 **$15.99**

Spiritual Manifestos: Visions for Renewed Religious Life in America from Young Spiritual Leaders of Many Faiths Edited by *Niles Elliot Goldstein; Preface by Martin E. Marty*
6 x 9, 256 pp, HC, 978-1-893361-09-6 **$21.95**

A Walk with Four Spiritual Guides: Krishna, Buddha, Jesus, and Ramakrishna
by *Andrew Harvey* 5½ x 8½, 192 pp, 10 b/w photos & illus., Quality PB, 978-1-59473-138-9 **$15.99**

What Matters: Spiritual Nourishment for Head and Heart
by *Frederick Franck* 5 x 7¼, 128 pp, 50+ b/w illus., HC, 978-1-59473-013-9 **$16.99**

Who Is My God?, 2nd Edition: An Innovative Guide to Finding Your Spiritual Identity
Created by *the Editors at SkyLight Paths* 6 x 9, 160 pp, Quality PB, 978-1-59473-014-6 **$15.99**

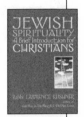

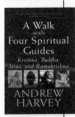

Spirituality—A Week Inside

Come and Sit: A Week Inside Meditation Centers
by *Marcia Z. Nelson; Foreword by Wayne Teasdale*
The insider's guide to meditation in a variety of different spiritual traditions—Buddhist, Hindu, Christian, Jewish, and Sufi traditions.
6 x 9, 224 pp, b/w photos, Quality PB, 978-1-893361-35-5 **$16.95**

Lighting the Lamp of Wisdom: A Week Inside a Yoga Ashram
by *John Ittner; Foreword by Dr. David Frawley*
This insider's guide to Hindu spiritual life takes you into a typical week of retreat inside a yoga ashram to demystify the experience and show you what to expect.
6 x 9, 192 pp, 10+ b/w photos, Quality PB, 978-1-893361-52-2 **$15.95**

Making a Heart for God: A Week Inside a Catholic Monastery
by *Dianne Aprile; Foreword by Brother Patrick Hart, ocso*
Takes you to the Abbey of Gethsemani—the Trappist monastery in Kentucky that was home to author Thomas Merton—to explore the details.
6 x 9, 224 pp, b/w photos, Quality PB, 978-1-893361-49-2 **$16.95**

Waking Up: A Week Inside a Zen Monastery
by *Jack Maguire; Foreword by John Daido Loori, Roshi*
An essential guide to what it's like to spend a week inside a Zen Buddhist monastery.
6 x 9, 224 pp, b/w photos, Quality PB, 978-1-893361-55-3 **$16.95**
HC, 978-1-893361-13-3 **$21.95**

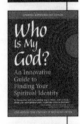

Children's Spirituality

Remembering My Grandparent: A Kid's Own Grief Workbook in the Christian Tradition *by Nechama Liss-Levinson, PhD, and Rev. Molly Phinney Baskette, MDiv*
8 x 10, 48 pp, 2-color text, HC, 978-1-59473-212-6 **$16.99** *For ages 7–13*

Does God Ever Sleep? *by Joan Sauro, CSJ; Full-color photos*
A charming nighttime reminder that God is always present in our lives.
10 x 8½, 32 pp, Quality PB, Full-color photos, 978-1-59473-110-5 **$8.99** *For ages 3–6*

Does God Forgive Me? *by August Gold; Full-color photos by Diane Hardy Waller*
Gently shows how God forgives all that we do if we are truly sorry.
10 x 8½, 32 pp, Quality PB, Full-color photos, 978-1-59473-142-6 **$8.99** *For ages 3–6*

God Said Amen *by Sandy Eisenberg Sasso; Full-color illus. by Avi Katz*
A warm and inspiring tale of two kingdoms that shows us that we need only reach out to each other to find the answers to our prayers.
9 x 12, 32 pp, HC, Full-color illus., 978-1-58023-080-3 **$16.95**
For ages 4 & up (a Jewish Lights book)

How Does God Listen? *by Kay Lindahl; Full-color photos by Cynthia Maloney*
How do we know when God is listening to us? Children will find the answers to these questions as they engage their senses while the story unfolds, learning how God listens in the wind, waves, clouds, hot chocolate, perfume, our tears and our laughter.
10 x 8½, 32 pp, Quality PB, Full-color photos, 978-1-59473-084-9 **$8.99** *For ages 3–6*

In God's Hands *by Lawrence Kushner and Gary Schmidt; Full-color illus. by Matthew J. Baeck*
9 x 12, 32 pp, Full-color illus., HC, 978-1-58023-224-1 **$16.99** *For ages 5 & up (a Jewish Lights book)*

In God's Name *by Sandy Eisenberg Sasso; Full-color illus. by Phoebe Stone*
Like an ancient myth in its poetic text and vibrant illustrations, this award-winning modern fable about the search for God's name celebrates the diversity and, at the same time, the unity of all the people of the world.
9 x 12, 32 pp, HC, Full-color illus., 978-1-879045-26-2 **$16.99**
For ages 4 & up (a Jewish Lights book)

Also available in Spanish: El nombre de Dios
9 x 12, 32 pp, HC, Full-color illus., 978-1-893361-63-8 **$16.95**

In Our Image: God's First Creatures
by Nancy Sohn Swartz; Full-color illus. by Melanie Hall
A playful new twist on the Genesis story—from the perspective of the animals. Celebrates the interconnectedness of nature and the harmony of all living things. 9 x 12, 32 pp, HC, Full-color illus., 978-1-879045-99-6 **$16.95**
For ages 4 & up (a Jewish Lights book)

Noah's Wife: The Story of Naamah
by Sandy Eisenberg Sasso; Full-color illus. by Bethanne Andersen
This new story, based on an ancient text, opens readers' religious imaginations to new ideas about the well-known story of the Flood. When God tells Noah to bring the animals of the world onto the ark, God also calls on Naamah, Noah's wife, to save each plant on Earth.
9 x 12, 32 pp, HC, Full-color illus., 978-1-58023-134-3 **$16.95**
For ages 4 & up (a Jewish Lights book)

Also available: Naamah: Noah's Wife (A Board Book)
by Sandy Eisenberg Sasso; Full-color illus. by Bethanne Andersen
5 x 5, 24 pp, Board Book, Full-color illus., 978-1-893361-56-0 **$7.99** *For ages 0–4*

Where Does God Live? *by August Gold and Matthew J. Perlman*
Using simple, everyday examples that children can relate to, this colorful book helps young readers develop a personal understanding of God.
10 x 8½, 32 pp, Quality PB, Full-color photo illus., 978-1-893361-39-3 **$8.99** *For ages 3–6*

Spiritual Biography—SkyLight Lives

SkyLight Lives reintroduces the lives and works of key spiritual figures of our time—people who by their teaching or example have challenged our assumptions about spirituality and have caused us to look at it in new ways.

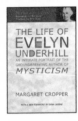 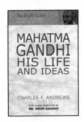  

The Life of Evelyn Underhill
An Intimate Portrait of the Groundbreaking Author of *Mysticism*
by Margaret Cropper; Foreword by Dana Greene
Evelyn Underhill was a passionate writer and teacher who wrote elegantly on mysticism, worship, and devotional life.
6 x 9, 288 pp, 5 b/w photos, Quality PB, 978-1-893361-70-6 **$18.95**

Mahatma Gandhi: His Life and Ideas
by Charles F. Andrews; Foreword by Dr. Arun Gandhi
Examines from a contemporary Christian activist's point of view the religious ideas and political dynamics that influenced the birth of the peaceful resistance movement.
6 x 9, 336 pp, 5 b/w photos, Quality PB, 978-1-893361-89-8 **$18.95**

Simone Weil: A Modern Pilgrimage
by Robert Coles
The extraordinary life of the spiritual philosopher who's been called both saint and madwoman.
6 x 9, 208 pp, Quality PB, 978-1-893361-34-8 **$16.95**

Zen Effects: The Life of Alan Watts
by Monica Furlong
Through his widely popular books and lectures, Alan Watts (1915–1973) did more to introduce Eastern philosophy and religion to Western minds than any figure before or since.
6 x 9, 264 pp, Quality PB, 978-1-893361-32-4 **$16.95**

More Spiritual Biography

Bede Griffiths: An Introduction to His Interspiritual Thought
by Wayne Teasdale
The first study of his contemplative experience and thought, exploring the intersection of Hinduism and Christianity.
6 x 9, 288 pp, Quality PB, 978-1-893361-77-5 **$18.95**

The Soul of the Story: Meetings with Remarkable People
by Rabbi David Zeller
Inspiring and entertaining, this compelling collection of spiritual adventures assures us that no spiritual lesson truly learned is ever lost.
6 x 9, 288 pp, HC, 978-1-58023-272-2 **$21.99** *(a Jewish Lights book)*

Sacred Texts—SkyLight Illuminations Series

Offers today's spiritual seeker an accessible entry into the great classic texts of the world's spiritual traditions. Each classic is presented in an accessible translation, with facing pages of guided commentary from experts, giving you the keys you need to understand the history, context and meaning of the text. This series enables you, whatever your background, to experience and understand classic spiritual texts directly, and to make them a part of your life.

CHRISTIANITY

The End of Days: Essential Selections from Apocalyptic Texts—Annotated & Explained *Annotation by Robert G. Clouse*
Helps you understand the complex Christian visions of the end of the world.
5½ x 8½, 224 pp, Quality PB, 978-1-59473-170-9 **$16.99**

The Hidden Gospel of Matthew: Annotated & Explained
Translation & Annotation by Ron Miller
Takes you deep into the text cherished around the world to discover the words and events that have the strongest connection to the historical Jesus.
5½ x 8½, 272 pp, Quality PB, 978-1-59473-038-2 **$16.99**

The Lost Sayings of Jesus: Teachings from Ancient Christian, Jewish, Gnostic and Islamic Sources—Annotated & Explained
Translation & Annotation by Andrew Phillip Smith; Foreword by Stephan A. Hoeller
This collection of more than three hundred sayings depicts Jesus as a Wisdom teacher who speaks to people of all faiths as a mystic and spiritual master.
5½ x 8½, 240 pp, Quality PB, 978-1-59473-172-3 **$16.99**

Philokalia: The Eastern Christian Spiritual Texts—Selections Annotated & Explained *Annotation by Allyne Smith; Translation by G. E. H. Palmer, Phillip Sherrard and Bishop Kallistos Ware*
The first approachable introduction to the wisdom of the Philokalia, which is the classic text of Eastern Christian spirituality.
5½ x 8½, 240 pp, Quality PB, 978-1-59473-103-7 **$16.99**

Spiritual Writings on Mary: Annotated & Explained
Annotation by Mary Ford-Grabowsky; Foreword by Andrew Harvey
Examines the role of Mary, the mother of Jesus, as a source of inspiration in history and in life today. 5½ x 8½, 288 pp, Quality PB, 978-1-59473-001-6 **$16.99**

The Way of a Pilgrim: The Jesus Prayer Journey—Annotated & Explained
Translation & Annotation by Gleb Pokrovsky; Foreword by Andrew Harvey
This classic of Russian spirituality is the delightful account of one man who sets out to learn the prayer of the heart, also known as the "Jesus prayer."
5½ x 8½, 160 pp, Illus., Quality PB, 978-1-893361-31-7 **$14.95**

MORMONISM

The Book of Mormon: Selections Annotated & Explained
Annotation by Jana Riess; Foreword by Phyllis Tickle
Explores the sacred epic that is cherished by more than twelve million members of the LDS church as the keystone of their faith.
5½ x 8½ , 272 pp, Quality PB, 978-1-59473-076-4 **$16.99**

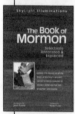

NATIVE AMERICAN

Native American Stories of the Sacred: Annotated & Explained
Retold & Annotated by Evan T. Pritchard
Intended for more than entertainment, these teaching tales contain elegantly simple illustrations of time-honored truths.
5½ x 8½, 272 pp, Quality PB, 978-1-59473-112-9 **$16.99**

Sacred Texts—cont.

GNOSTICISM

The Gospel of Philip: Annotated & Explained
Translation & Annotation by Andrew Phillip Smith; Foreword by Stevan Davies
Reveals otherwise unrecorded sayings of Jesus and fragments of Gnostic mythology.
5½ x 8½, 160 pp, Quality PB, 978-1-59473-111-2 **$16.99**

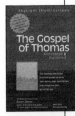

The Gospel of Thomas: Annotated & Explained
Translation & Annotation by Stevan Davies Sheds new light on the origins of Christianity and portrays Jesus as a wisdom-loving sage. 5½ x 8½, 192 pp, Quality PB, 978-1-893361-45-4 **$16.99**

The Secret Book of John: The Gnostic Gospel—Annotated & Explained
Translation & Annotation by Stevan Davies The most significant and influential text of the ancient Gnostic religion. 5½ x 8½, 208 pp, Quality PB, 978-1-59473-082-5 **$16.99**

JUDAISM

The Divine Feminine in Biblical Wisdom Literature
Selections Annotated & Explained
Translation & Annotation by Rabbi Rami Shapiro; Foreword by Rev. Cynthia Bourgeault, PhD
Uses the Hebrew books of Psalms, Proverbs, Song of Songs, Ecclesiastes and Job, Wisdom literature and the Wisdom of Solomon to clarify who Wisdom is.
5½ x 8½, 240 pp, Quality PB, 978-1-59473-109-9 **$16.99**

Ethics of the Sages: *Pirke Avot*—Annotated & Explained
Translation & Annotation by Rabbi Rami Shapiro Clarifies the ethical teachings of the early Rabbis. 5½ x 8½, 192 pp, Quality PB, 978-1-59473-207-2 **$16.99**

Hasidic Tales: Annotated & Explained
Translation & Annotation by Rabbi Rami Shapiro
Introduces the legendary tales of the impassioned Hasidic rabbis, presenting them as stories rather than as parables. 5½ x 8½, 240 pp, Quality PB, 978-1-893361-86-7 **$16.95**

The Hebrew Prophets: Selections Annotated & Explained
Translation & Annotation by Rabbi Rami Shapiro; Foreword by Zalman M. Schachter-Shalomi
Focuses on the central themes covered by all the Hebrew prophets.
5½ x 8½, 224 pp, Quality PB, 978-1-59473-037-5 **$16.99**

Zohar: Annotated & Explained *Translation & Annotation by Daniel C. Matt*
The best-selling author of *The Essential Kabbalah* brings together in one place the most important teachings of the Zohar, the canonical text of Jewish mystical tradition.
5½ x 8½, 176 pp, Quality PB, 978-1-893361-51-5 **$15.99**

EASTERN RELIGIONS

Bhagavad Gita: Annotated & Explained *Translation by Shri Purohit Swami*
Annotation by Kendra Crossen Burroughs Explains references and philosophical terms, shares the interpretations of famous spiritual leaders and scholars, and more.
5½ x 8½, 192 pp, Quality PB, 978-1-893361-28-7 **$16.95**

Dhammapada: Annotated & Explained *Translation by Max Müller and revised by Jack Maguire; Annotation by Jack Maguire* Contains all of Buddhism's key teachings.
5½ x 8½, 160 pp, b/w photos, Quality PB, 978-1-893361-42-3 **$14.95**

Rumi and Islam: Selections from His Stories, Poems, and Discourses—
Annotated & Explained *Translation & Annotation by Ibrahim Gamard*
Focuses on Rumi's place within the Sufi tradition of Islam, providing insight into the mystical side of the religion. 5½ x 8½, 240 pp, Quality PB, 978-1-59473-002-3 **$15.99**

Selections from the Gospel of Sri Ramakrishna: Annotated & Explained
Translation by Swami Nikhilananda; Annotation by Kendra Crossen Burroughs
Introduces the fascinating world of the Indian mystic and the universal appeal of his message. 5½ x 8½, 240 pp, b/w photos, Quality PB, 978-1-893361-46-1 **$16.95**

Tao Te Ching: Annotated & Explained *Translation & Annotation by Derek Lin*
Foreword by Lama Surya Das Introduces an Eastern classic in an accessible, poetic and completely original way. 5½ x 8½, 192 pp, Quality PB, 978-1-59473-204-1 **$16.99**

Spirituality of the Seasons

Autumn: A Spiritual Biography of the Season
Edited by Gary Schmidt and Susan M. Felch; Illustrations by Mary Azarian
Rejoice in autumn as a time of preparation and reflection. Includes Wendell Berry, David James Duncan, Robert Frost, A. Bartlett Giamatti, E. B. White, P. D. James, Julian of Norwich, Garret Keizer, Tracy Kidder, Anne Lamott, May Sarton.
6 x 9, 320 pp, 5 b/w illus., Quality PB, 978-1-59473-118-1 **$18.99**
HC, 978-1-59473-005-4 **$22.99**

Spring: A Spiritual Biography of the Season
Edited by Gary Schmidt and Susan M. Felch; Illustrations by Mary Azarian
Explore the gentle unfurling of spring and reflect on how nature celebrates rebirth and renewal. Includes Jane Kenyon, Lucy Larcom, Harry Thurston, Nathaniel Hawthorne, Noel Perrin, Annie Dillard, Martha Ballard, Barbara Kingsolver, Dorothy Wordsworth, Donald Hall, David Brill, Lionel Basney, Isak Dinesen, Paul Laurence Dunbar. 6 x 9, 352 pp, 6 b/w illus., HC, 978-1-59473-114-3 **$21.99**

Summer: A Spiritual Biography of the Season
Edited by Gary Schmidt and Susan M. Felch; Illustrations by Barry Moser
"A sumptuous banquet.... These selections lift up an exquisite wholeness found within an everyday sophistication."— ★ *Publishers Weekly* starred review
Includes Anne Lamott, Luci Shaw, Ray Bradbury, Richard Selzer, Thomas Lynch, Walt Whitman, Carl Sandburg, Sherman Alexie, Madeleine L'Engle, Jamaica Kincaid.
6 x 9, 304 pp, 5 b/w illus., Quality PB, 978-1-59473-183-9 **$18.99**
HC, 978-1-59473-083-2 **$21.99**

Winter: A Spiritual Biography of the Season
Edited by Gary Schmidt and Susan M. Felch; Illustrations by Barry Moser
"This outstanding anthology features top-flight nature and spirituality writers on the fierce, inexorable season of winter.... Remarkably lively and warm, despite the icy subject." — ★ *Publishers Weekly* starred review
Includes Will Campbell, Rachel Carson, Annie Dillard, Donald Hall, Ron Hansen, Jane Kenyon, Jamaica Kincaid, Barry Lopez, Kathleen Norris, John Updike, E. B. White.
6 x 9, 288 pp, 6 b/w illus., Deluxe PB w/flaps, 978-1-893361-92-8 **$18.95**
HC, 978-1-893361-53-9 **$21.95**

Spirituality / Animal Companions

Blessing the Animals: Prayers and Ceremonies to Celebrate God's Creatures, Wild and Tame *Edited by Lynn L. Caruso* 5 x 7¼, 256 pp, HC, 978-1-59473-145-7 **$19.99**

What Animals Can Teach Us about Spirituality: Inspiring Lessons from Wild and Tame Creatures *by Diana L. Guerrero* 6 x 9, 176 pp, Quality PB, 978-1-893361-84-3 **$16.95**

Spirituality

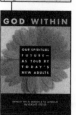

Awakening the Spirit, Inspiring the Soul
30 Stories of Interspiritual Discovery in the Community of Faiths
Edited by Brother Wayne Teasdale and Martha Howard, MD; Foreword by Joan Borysenko, PhD
Thirty original spiritual mini-autobiographies showcase the varied ways that people come to faith—and what that means—in today's multi-religious world.
6 x 9, 224 pp, HC, 978-1-59473-039-0 **$21.99**

The Alphabet of Paradise: An A–Z of Spirituality for Everyday Life
by Howard Cooper 5 x 7¼, 224 pp, Quality PB, 978-1-893361-80-5 **$16.95**

Creating a Spiritual Retirement: A Guide to the Unseen Possibilities in Our Lives
by Molly Srode 6 x 9, 208 pp, b/w photos, Quality PB, 978-1-59473-050-4 **$14.99**
HC, 978-1-893361-75-1 **$19.95**

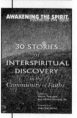

Finding Hope: Cultivating God's Gift of a Hopeful Spirit
by Marcia Ford 8 x 8, 200 pp, Quality PB, 978-1-59473-211-9 **$16.99**

The Geography of Faith: Underground Conversations on Religious, Political and Social Change *by Daniel Berrigan and Robert Coles* 6 x 9, 224 pp, Quality PB, 978-1-893361-40-9 **$16.95**

God Within: Our Spiritual Future—As Told by Today's New Adults *Edited by Jon M. Sweeney and the Editors at SkyLight Paths* 6 x 9, 176 pp, Quality PB, 978-1-893361-15-7 **$14.95**

Spirituality & Crafts

The Knitting Way: A Guide to Spiritual Self-Discovery
by Linda Skolnik and Janice MacDaniels
7 x 9, 240 pp, Quality PB, b/w photographs, 978-1-59473-079-5 **$16.99**

The Quilting Path: A Guide to Spiritual Discovery through Fabric, Thread and Kabbalah
by Louise Silk
7 x 9, 192 pp, Quality PB, b/w photographs and illustrations, 978-1-59473-206-5 **$16.99**

The Scrapbooking Journey: A Hands-On Guide to Spiritual Discovery
by Cory Richardson-Lauve; Foreword by Stacy Julian
7 x 9, 176 pp, Quality PB, 8-page full-color insert, plus b/w photographs
978-1-59473-216-4 **$18.99**

Spiritual Practice

Divining the Body: Reclaim the Holiness of Your Physical Self
by Jan Phillips
A practical and inspiring guidebook for connecting the body and soul in spiritual practice. Leads you into a milieu of reverence, mystery and delight, helping you discover your body as a pathway to the Divine.
8 x 8, 256 pp, Quality PB, 978-1-59473-080-1 **$16.99**

Finding Time for the Timeless: Spirituality in the Workweek
by John McQuiston II
Simple, refreshing stories that provide you with examples of how you can refocus and enrich your daily life using prayer or meditation, ritual and other forms of spiritual practice. 5½ x 6¾, 208 pp, HC, 978-1-59473-035-1 **$17.99**

The Gospel of Thomas: A Guidebook for Spiritual Practice
by Ron Miller; Translations by Stevan Davies
An innovative guide to bring a new spiritual classic into daily life.
6 x 9, 160 pp, Quality PB, 978-1-59473-047-4 **$14.99**

Earth, Water, Fire, and Air: Essential Ways of Connecting to Spirit
by Cait Johnson 6 x 9, 224 pp, HC, 978-1-893361-65-2 **$19.95**

Labyrinths from the Outside In: Walking to Spiritual Insight—A Beginner's Guide
by Donna Schaper and Carole Ann Camp
6 x 9, 208 pp, b/w illus. and photos, Quality PB, 978-1-893361-18-8 **$16.95**

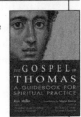

Practicing the Sacred Art of Listening: A Guide to Enrich Your Relationships and Kindle Your Spiritual Life—The Listening Center Workshop
by Kay Lindahl 8 x 8, 176 pp, Quality PB, 978-1-893361-85-0 **$16.95**

Releasing the Creative Spirit: Unleash the Creativity in Your Life
by Dan Wakefield 7 x 10, 256 pp, Quality PB, 978-1-893361-36-2 **$16.95**

The Sacred Art of Bowing: Preparing to Practice
by Andi Young 5½ x 8½, 128 pp, b/w illus., Quality PB, 978-1-893361-82-9 **$14.95**

The Sacred Art of Chant: Preparing to Practice
by Ana Hernández 5½ x 8½, 192 pp, Quality PB, 978-1-59473-036-8 **$15.99**

The Sacred Art of Fasting: Preparing to Practice
by Thomas Ryan, CSP 5½ x 8½, 192 pp, Quality PB, 978-1-59473-078-8 **$15.99**

The Sacred Art of Forgiveness: Forgiving Ourselves and Others through God's Grace
by Marcia Ford 8 x 8, 176 pp, Quality PB, 978-1-59473-175-4 **$16.99**

The Sacred Art of Listening: Forty Reflections for Cultivating a Spiritual Practice
by Kay Lindahl; Illustrations by Amy Schnapper
8 x 8, 160 pp, b/w illus., Quality PB, 978-1-893361-44-7 **$16.99**

The Sacred Art of Lovingkindness: Preparing to Practice
by Rabbi Rami Shapiro; Foreword by Marcia Ford
5½ x 8½, 176 pp, Quality PB, 978-1-59473-151-8 **$16.99**

Sacred Speech: A Practical Guide for Keeping Spirit in Your Speech
by Rev. Donna Schaper 6 x 9, 176 pp, Quality PB, 978-1-59473-068-9 **$15.99**
HC, 978-1-893361-74-4 **$21.95**

About SKYLIGHT PATHS Publishing

SkyLight Paths Publishing is creating a place where people of different spiritual traditions come together for challenge and inspiration, a place where we can help each other understand the mystery that lies at the heart of our existence.

Through spirituality, our religious beliefs are increasingly becoming a part of our lives—rather than *apart* from our lives. While many of us may be more interested than ever in spiritual growth, we may be less firmly planted in traditional religion. Yet, we do want to deepen our relationship to the sacred, to learn from our own as well as from other faith traditions, and to practice in new ways.

SkyLight Paths sees both believers and seekers as a community that increasingly transcends traditional boundaries of religion and denomination—people wanting to learn from each other, *walking together, finding the way.*

For your information and convenience, at the back of this book we have provided a list of other SkyLight Paths books you might find interesting and useful. They cover the following subjects:

Buddhism / Zen	Gnosticism	Mysticism
Catholicism	Hinduism /	Poetry
Children's Books	Vedanta	Prayer
Christianity	Inspiration	Religious Etiquette
Comparative	Islam / Sufism	Retirement
Religion	Judaism / Kabbalah /	Spiritual Biography
Current Events	Enneagram	Spiritual Direction
Earth-Based	Meditation	Spirituality
Spirituality	Midrash Fiction	Women's Interest
Global Spiritual	Monasticism	Worship
Perspectives		

Or phone, fax, mail or e-mail to: SKYLIGHT PATHS Publishing
Sunset Farm Offices, Route 4 • P.O. Box 237 • Woodstock, Vermont 05091
Tel: (802) 457-4000 • Fax: (802) 457-4004 • www.skylightpaths.com
Credit card orders: (800) 962-4544 (8:30AM–5:30PM ET Monday–Friday)
Generous discounts on quantity orders. SATISFACTION GUARANTEED. Prices subject to change.

**For more information about each book,
visit our website at www.skylightpaths.com**